Exploring
CANYONLANDS
AND ARCHES
National Parks

Published in cooperation with the **National Park Service,**
the **Canyonlands Natural History Association,**
and **Trails Illustrated Maps**

Bill Schneider

FALCON®

Guilford, Connecticut
An imprint of The Globe Pequot Press

All black-and-white photos by author.
Front cover photo by Cathy and Gordon Illg; back cover photos (lower) Erik Molvar, (upper) Pat and Chuck Blackley

Library of Congress Cataloging-in-Publication Data

Schneider, Bill.
        Exploring Canyonlands and Arches national parks / Bill Schneider.
                p. cm.
        "Published in partnership with the National Park Service, the Canyonlands Natural History Association, and Trails Illustrated Maps."
        ISBN 1-56044-510-6 (pbk.)
        1. Canyonlands National Park (Utah)—Guidebooks. 2. Arches National Park (Utah)—Guidebooks. 3. Hiking—Utah—Canyonlands National Park—Guidebooks. 4. Hiking—Utah—Arches National Park—Guidebooks. 5. Automobile travel—Utah—Canyonlands National Park—Guidebooks. 6. Automobile travel—Utah—Arches National Park—Guidebooks. I. Title.
F832.C37S36 1997
917.92'59—dc21   96-50439
                                                      CIP

♻ Text pages printed on recycled paper.
Manufactured in the United States of America
First Edition/Eighth Printing

CAUTION
Outdoor recreational activities are by their very nature potentially hazardous. All participants in such activities must assume the responsibility for their own actions and safety. The information contained in this guidebook cannot replace sound judgment and good decision–making skills, which help reduce risk exposure, nor does the scope of this book allow for disclosure of all the potential hazards and risks involved in such activities.

Learn as much as possible about the outdoor recreational activities in which you participate, prepare for the unexpected, and be cautious. The reward will be a safer and more enjoyable experience.

"The land here is like a great book or a great symphony; it invites approaches toward comprehension on many levels, from all directions."

—Edward Abbey

BOOKS BY THE AUTHOR

Where the Grizzly Walks

The Dakota Image

Hiking Montana

The Yellowstone River

The Tree Giants

The Flight of the Nez Perce

Hiking the Beartooths

*Hiking Carlsbad Caverns and
Guadalupe Mountains National Parks*

Bear Aware

*Best Easy Day Hikes
Arches and Canyonlands*

Hiking Yellowstone

*Best Easy Day Hikes
Yellowstone*

CONTENTS

CONTENTS

CANYONLANDS NATIONAL PARK
ISLAND IN THE SKY

CONTENTS

CONTENTS

ACKNOWLEDGMENTS

This trail guide was a major cooperative effort between the National park Service staff at Canyonlands and Arches national parks and the staff of the Canyonlands Natural History Association. It would be most appropriate to say that it would not have happened without them.

There were more people helping out that I could list here, but I would especially like to thank these NPS employees who helped coordinate, research and review this guidebook—Larry Frederick, Bruce McCabe, Mary Beth Maynard, Karen Schlom, Cary Cox, Diane Allen and Fred Patton. Also, many thanks to Canyonlands Natural History Association employees Jean Treadway, Brad Wallis and Gloria Brown for their help in the project. And of course, thanks to Bill and Mary Kay Stoehr at Trails Illustrated Maps for providing the maps for the book.

As always, the staff at Falcon deserves a big thank you for putting up with my distractions while researching and writing the book with special thanks to Randall Green, our guidebook editor, Marita Martiniak, the graphic artist who laid out the book, Noelle Sullivan, the copy editor, and Tony Moore who did the elevation charts and overview maps.

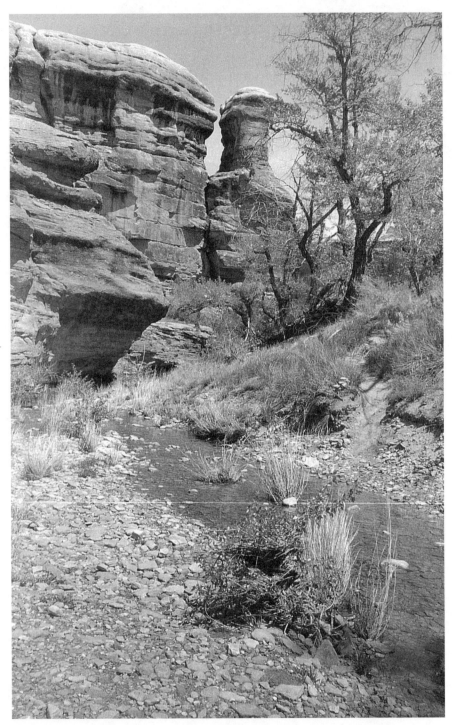

The trails of Arches and Canyonlands national parks often wind through gorgeous canyons such as Lost Canyon in the Needles District.

PREFACE: WHAT IS THE CANYONLANDS?

Geographically, The Canyonlands is a section of southeastern Utah, some of it embodied in two magnificent national parks, Arches and Canyonlands. But geography is only a small part of the story. Naturally, the Canyonlands is much more.

It's a rugged pinyon pine growing out of solid slickrock—and the beautiful blue pinyon jay screaming at you from it.

It's the stealthy mountain lion stalking the understandably skittish mule deer or the seldom-seen bobcat getting fat on the foolish young of the desert cottontail. You rarely see the desert cats, but they leave their story in the sand.

It's those little whiptail and fence lizards darting away as you walk down the trail. I wonder if a scientist will ever figure out how the little lizards can run so fast on one-quarter-inch legs?

It's those amazingly hardy desert plants. After being out in the Canyonlands heat a few days, you grow to really appreciate their toughness and special adaptations and longevity. Stepping on a desert plant is like cutting down a big tree in the rain forest—except the desert plant is probably older.

It's all that blackbrush, everywhere, like oceans of tumbleweeds that haven't blown away yet, growing on the harshest sites where only the hardiest plants could survive. Individual plants live for hundreds of years on almost nothing, and the desert bighorn will never have a food shortage.

It's a whole lot of slickrock, everywhere you look. Even when you aren't standing on it, you get the feeling it's only 2 or 3 inches down. Since lots of names get changed and shortened as time goes by, I suspect that slickrock is really a shortened version of slick-when-wet-rock.

It's those little potholes in the slickrock that evolve into micro-habitats and then into stone-ringed "pothole gardens," like bonsai gardens with all plants aged but dwarfed.

It's deep canyons winding aimlessly through the plateau and majestic arches highlighting so many skylines, along with awesome sandstone spires and cliffs, everywhere, and, of course, it's those "Canyonlands mushrooms," multi-hued, mushroom-shaped sandstone formations.

It's the light, that wonderfully clear light. The light can change colors of cliffs and highlight the gorgeous deep green of emerging buck thorn leaves against the reddish sandstone, especially on a rare overcast day or after a rain.

It's the quiet. I don't know why, but canyons always seems so quiet—at least compared to the forest or the beach or the prairie. Not even the wind seems to break the ever-present silence. And when there is a sound, you really hear it. When you sneeze, it echoes around for several seconds and you feel like saying, "Excuse me, Mother Nature." If you're lucky enough to get caught by an afternoon storm, you can hear the quiet burst suddenly with thunder that pounds up and down the canyon like a drum roll loud enough to shake off the desert varnish.

It's a classroom for prehistory—ancient rock art on canyon walls and adobe ruins under sandstone overhangs left by long-gone cultures. We have to paint our houses every few years, but these cultures painted their life story on desert rocks, and it has lasted two thousand years.

It's getting caught in a desert rain and sitting in an alcove to watch the rocks change color and the water system start to work—little rivulets following slickrock curves, merging, getting bigger and bigger. Those stark, dry pour-overs become gorgeous waterfalls right before your eyes, and the head of the newly born and very temporary stream inches its way down the dry wash. The rain washes dust off the plants, and they glow a vivid green and seem to almost get up and stretch like we do at the start of a new day.

It's the awesome flash flood that I haven't seen. . . yet. But I've seen the tracks a flash flood leaves, and I've talked to a few people fortunate enough to experience a flash flood ripping down a canyon. I'll keep coming back, hoping to see one.

Recreationally, the Canyonlands is a mecca for outdoor sports, but it's their natural wonders that make the hiking, mountain biking, four-wheeling, and river floating so great. In any geographic area, such outdoor sports are a lesson in self-denial, but in the Canyonlands, they also teach self-reliance.

Perhaps most of all, however, the Canyonlands is a place to relax, take a deep breath, let your fingernails grow. Do yourself a favor and don't hurry through the Canyonlands, seeing only a few arches, then moving on to the next national park. Instead, take your time and let the nature of the Canyonlands sneak up on you and forever wrap itself around your insides. This can become quite a burden, though—you'll become so attached to the place that you'll have to return again and again and again.

OVERVIEW MAP

LEGEND

	Interstate		Interstate Highway
	US Highway		Paved Road
	State or Other Principal Road		Unpaved Road
			4-wheel-drive Road

N

0   5   10
Miles

To 6

Green River

Crescent Junction

To Grand Junction, CO

Cisco

70

128

Green

River

191

Devils Garden

ARCHES NATIONAL PARK

Fisher Towers

The Windows

128

313

279

Moab

River

191

CANYONLANDS

Island in the Sky

To Hanksville

GLEN CANYON NRA

NATIONAL

Grand View Point

Needles Overlook (B.L.M.)

La Sal Jct.

The Maze

Hans Flat

PARK

Colorado

Needles

211

191

To Hite

Newspaper Rock

To Monticello

WHERE TO GO?

TYPE OF RECREATION	ARCHES	NEEDLES	ISLAND IN THE SKY	MAZE	OUTSIDE PARKS
MOUNTAIN BIKING *on backcountry roads*		●	●	●	●
MOUNTAIN BIKING *on single track trails*					●
HIKING *short, easy hiking trails*	●	●	●		
HIKING *moderate hiking trails*	●	●			
HIKING *long hiking trails*		●	●		
HIKING *off-trail routes*				●	
BACKPACKING		●	●	●	●
VEHICLE CAMPING *primitive campsites*		●	●	●	●
VEHICLE CAMPING *developed campgrounds*	●	●	●		●
SCENIC DRIVING AND SIGHTSEEING *paved roads*	●	●	●		●
FOUR-WHEELING *backcountry roads*		●	●	●	●

NOTE: This chart is only a general guide. You can, for example, find short hiking trails in all four regions of the parks. This chart only reflects the general suitability of each area to various forms of outdoor recreation.

INTRODUCTION: WHERE TO GO?

The area encompassed by Arches and Canyonlands national parks is a big place. So if you're heading for Arches and Canyonlands for the first time, where do you go?

It depends on how you like to enjoy the great outdoors. Mountain bikers, for example, might like the areas contiguous to the parks where they have more options. Ditto for four-wheel-drive fans. But here, unlike most national parks, you can also find opportunities for mountain biking and four-wheeling within park boundaries. If you're a hiker, you have lots of choices, depending on how much time you have, your physical capabilities, and how much adventure you want. For the adventuresome, it's the Maze, but for the beginner, it's Arches. For the casual tourist who wants to see some fantastic scenery without working up a sweat, it's the Island in the Sky or Arches.

The following list of general guidelines might make planning slightly easier, but to get more details to help with your decision on where to go, refer to the overview sections in each of the four major areas covered in this book—Arches National Park and the Needles, Island in the Sky and Maze districts of Canyonlands National Park. (The Orange Cliffs Unit of Glen Canyon National Recreation Area is included in the Maze District.)

Wherever you go, however, you are not likely to be disappointed.

PLANNING YOUR TRIP

Getting to Canyonlands or Arches national parks isn't a short drive for many people. It usually takes a major effort to get there, so plan your trip so you won't get stressed out or disappointed by some snafu that could have been avoided with advance planning.

As of January 1995, along with the publication of the new backcountry management plan for Canyonlands National Park, the National Park Service launched a reservation system for backcountry permits. You don't have to get a permit until you get to the park, but if you want to be sure you can actually camp in the campsite you've pre-selected, you should use the advance reservation system to make sure you can get a permit for that site. Demand for permits continues to increase, especially during spring and fall and at popular sites, so take advantage of the new system to avoid disappointment. Arches National Park is not covered by the backcountry management plan.

Before you apply for permits, digest as much information as you can about the area you plan to visit. Study the map and read whatever information you can get on the area. This saves you and the NPS time and frustration.

GETTING A BACKCOUNTRY PERMIT

Canyonlands National Park requires permits for backpacking, backcountry vehicle sites, mountain bike camping in all vehicle campsites and day use in three areas in the Needles District (Salt Creek, Horse Canyon, and Lavender Canyon). In most cases, no permit is required for day use.

The first step is to plan your trip. Call the park reservation office and request a backcountry trip planning guide, a free handout that will answer most of your questions. Then, as far in advance of your trip start date as possible (months if possible), request your reservations by mail or fax. If you plan a trip on the White Rim Road, you should make your reservation at least six months in advance. You can't make reservations over the phone, but you can call for help. All requests for advance reservations must include:

- Name and address of trip leader with phone numbers.
- Dates and campsites or zones desired with alternatives for both.
- The number of people in your group.
- The number of vehicles in your group (for vehicle campers only).
- The non-refundable permit fee.

You can pay for your permit with VISA or MASTERCARD or with a personal check or money order made payable to Canyonlands National Park. If faxing your reservation information, use credit card to pay. Please do not send cash.

Send a detailed itinerary with alternative sites, and a check or money order or your credit car number and expiration date to pay for the permit. Send the request to:

Reservation Office
Canyonlands National Park
2282 South West Resource Blvd.
Moab, UT 84532.

Phone: (801) 259-4351
FAX: (435) 259-4285
Recorded information: (801) 259-4285
Website address: www.nps.gov/cany/

The NPS will respond to both phone or mail requests and send a written confirmation. This confirmation is **not** your permit. You must pick up the permit at the visitor center in the district where the trip begins. If you have to cancel or change your trip, please notify the Reservation Office as soon as possible so the campsite(s) can be made available to other park visitors.

If the campsite you want has already been reserved, the NPS will try to get as close to your route as possible by reserving alternative sites. If you send your alternatives, it makes it easier for the NPS to schedule something close to the trip you have planned. If you're already in the park, you can apply for your permit in person and pay the fee at that time. However, in some cases, the area you want to see might not have permits available, especially during peak seasons.

FEES

Fees can change from time to time, but when this book was published the NPS had established the following fees:

$10 — Backpacking permits
$25 — Backcountry vehicle or mountain biking campsites

Incidentally, reservation fees do not go into the general fund in Washington, D.C. These fees stay in Canyonlands National Park and pay for the operation of the backcountry reservation system. The fees cover the expense of salaries, phone lines, office supplies, postage, publication of a trip planner, and maintenance of the computer system. Without these fees, the reservation system would be impossible, and permits would be issued on a first-come, first-served basis.

OTHER CAMPING OPTIONS

If you want to stay in developed campgrounds, you can try the following campgrounds:

Devils Garden Campground — Arches National Park, 50 sites plus 2 group sites, water available peak season (mid-March through October), $10 fee in season, $5 fee in winter, maximum group size limit 10 people per site with the exception of the group sites.

Squaw Flat Campground — Needles District, 26 sites plus 3 group sites, drinking water available mid-March through October, $8 per night fee, maximum group size limit 10 people per site with the exception of the group sites.

Willow Flat Campground — Island in the Sky District, 12 sites, no fee, no water, maximum group size 10 people/site.

In peak seasons, these national park campgrounds fill up fast, and spaces go on a first-come, first-served basis with the exception of the group sites, which can be reserved. The ranger on duty at the entrance station often can tell you how full a campground is. Fees subject to change without notice.

Dead Horse Point State Park near the Island in the Sky District also has a 21-site campground. You can reserve a site in advance by calling Utah State Parks at 800-322-3770.

If you can't get a backcountry permit or for some reason don't want to stay in the national parks, you can often find a place outside of the parks on public land managed by the Bureau of Land Management and the USDA Forest Service. There are also private campgrounds around the Needles and Moab areas, and you can get information on these campsites by calling the local travel council. To get more information on these camping alternatives, call the following phone numbers:

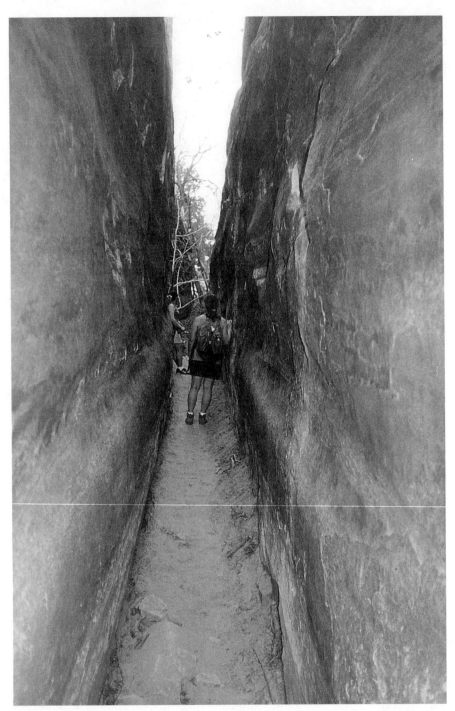

Several trails in both parks go through "joints" between sandstone formations such as this one in the first part of the trail to Chesler Park in the Needles District.

Bureau of Land Management Offices:
Moab Office (outside Island in the Sky) — (801) 259-6111
San Juan Resource Area (outside Needles) — (801) 587-2141
Hanksville Resource Area (outside the Maze) — (801) 542-3461

USDA Forest Service Offices:
(801) 259-7155

Travel Councils:
Grand County (Moab/Green River) — (800) 635-6622
San Juan County (Monticello/Blanding) — (800) 574-4386

WHERE TO GET WATER

When you head for Arches or Canyonlands national parks, bring plenty of water with you (one gallon per person per day, stored in multiple containers). But if you have to load up on water when you get to the parks, you can find water at these locations:

Arches National Park — Visitor Center, year-round and Devils Garden Campground and Trailhead, mid-March through October.
Island in the Sky District — Visitor Center (for sale by the gallon).
Needles District — Visitor Center and Squaw Flat Campground.
Maze — No water available in the Maze.

In a few places in Canyonlands National Park, you hike on short sections of road, such as this section of the Confluence Overlook Trail in the Needles District.

FINDING MAPS

Good maps are easy to find, and they are essential to any wilderness trip. For safety reasons, you need maps for route-finding and for "staying found." For non-safety reasons, you would not want to miss out on the joy of whittling away hours staring at a topo map and wondering what it really looks like here and there.

For trips into the Canyonlands and Arches national parks, you have two good choices for maps—U.S. Geological Survey (USGS) topo maps and Trails Illustrated maps. Well-prepared wilderness travelers take both. You can find these maps at the following locations:

Trails Illustrated Maps—Check at the national park visitor centers when you get to the parks or gift shops and bookstores in the local area. If you would like to get the maps in advance, you can order them directly from Falcon Press Publishing by calling 1-800-582-2665.

USGS Maps—These maps are also available at national park visitor centers and sporting goods stores in the local area. Again, if you would like the maps in advance, write directly to the USGS at the following address:

> Map Distribution
> U.S. Geological Survey
> Box 25286, Federal Center
> Denver, CO 80225

To make sure you order the correct USGS map, refer to the grid on the opposite page.

FOR MORE INFORMATION

The best source of more information is the National Park Service. In most cases you can get the information you need at the headquarters for each park, at the following addresses and phone numbers:

Arches National Park
P.O. Box 907
Moab, UT 84532

Phone: (801) 259-8161 (voice)
(801) 259-5279 (TTY)

Canyonlands National Park
2282 South West Resource Blvd.
Moab, UT 84532

Phone: (801) 259-7164

CANYONLANDS NATURAL HISTORY ASSOCIATION

Canyonlands Natural History Association is a not-for-profit organization established to assist the educational and scientific efforts of the National Park Service (NPS), Bureau of Land Management (BLM) and USDA Forest Service (USFS) in southeastern Utah. CNHA's goal is to enhance each visitor's appreciation of public lands by providing quality educational materials, both free and for sale in agency visitor centers. All sales items have been approved after a rigorous review process managed by CNHA and the three federal agencies.

Bookstore and mail order sales are CNHA's primary source of income, and proceeds support the agencies' programs in various ways, including sales and free publications, seminars, outdoor education programs for Moab schools, equipment and supplies for rangers/naturalists, exhibits, new facilities, and research funds.

You can help the Association in efforts to preserve the parks and surrounding public lands by purchasing items in Association bookstores, with direct donations, or by becoming a member. You can get more information on Canyonlands Natural History Association at the Moab Information Center, any park visitor center or contacting them at this phone and address:

Canyonlands Natural History Association
3031 South Highway 191
Moab, UT 84532

Phone: (801) 259-6003
Fax: (801) 259-8263
e-mail: www.moabutah.com/cnha/
Toll Free: 1-800-840-8978

Key to Unpaved Roads in Canyonlands and Arches

	2WD-LC	2WD-HC	4WD-LC	4WD-HC
ARCHES	Salt Valley		Willow Flats	Four-Wheel-Drive Road
ISLAND IN THE SKY	Green River Overlook			Shafer Trail, Taylor Canyon, White Rim Road, Lathrop Canyon
NEEDLES	Elephant Hill (to the trailhead) Cave Spring			Colorado Overlook, Salt Creek, Horse Canyon, Lavender Canyon, Elephant Hill, Devils Lane
MAZE		Horsehoe Canyon, Gordon Flats, Waterhole Flat, Hite		Doll House, Millard Canyon, Maze Overlook, North Point, Panorama Point, Cleopatra's Chair, Big Ridge, Sunset Pass, Golden Stairs

Definitions: 2WD (two-wheel drive); 4WD (four-wheel drive); HC (high clearance); LC (low clearance)

Key to Trails in Canyonlands and Arches

	EASY DAY HIKES	MODERATE DAY HIKES	DIFFICULT DAY HIKES	MULTI- DAY HIKES
ARCHES	Desert Nature Trail, Windows Primitive Loop, Park Avenue, Sand Dune Arch, Broken Arch, Balanced Rock, Skyline Arch, Double Arch, Devils Garden (to Landscape Arch)	Devils Garden (to Double O Arch), Delicate Arch, Tower Arch, Fiery Furnace	Fiery Furnace, Devils Garden Loop	
ISLAND	Lathrop (to rim), Mesa Arch, Murphy Point, White Rim Overlook, Grand View, Gooseneck	Neck Spring, Lathrop (to White Rim Road), Aztec Butte, Whale Rock, Upheaval Dome Overlook, Fort Bottom, Up- heaval Canyon, Moses	Lathrop (to Colorado River), Wilhite Alcove Spring, Syncline Loop, Murphy Basin, Gooseberry, Upheaval Canyon	Lathrop (to Colorado River) Wilhite, Alcove Spring, Alcove Spring/Syncline Loop, Syncline Loop, Murphy Basin, Goose- berry, Up- heaval Canyon
NEEDLES	Roadside Ruin, Pothole Point, Angel Arch, Castle Arch, Fortress Arch, Cave Spring, Slickrock Foot Trail	The Joint Trail, Druid Arch, Druid Arch West, Chesler Park Loop, Devils Pocket Loop, Elephant Hill to Squaw Canyon, Squaw Canyon/ Big Spring Canyon	Peekaboo, Big Spring Canyon/ Elephant Canyon, Lost Canyon, Lower Red Lake, Confluence Overlook, Upper Salt Creek	Upper Salt Creek, Big Needles, Chesler Park/ Devils Kitchen, Peekaboo, Lost Canyon, Lower Red Lake, Lost Canyon/Elephant Canyon, Squaw Canyon/Big Spring Canyon, Big Spring Canyon/Elephant Canyon, Druid Arch, Druid Arch West, Chesler Park, Devils Pocket Loop
MAZE	Granary	Golden Stairs, Happy Canyon, Spanish Bottom, Great Gallery, Colorado/Green River Overlook	Harvest Scene, North Trail, Maze Overlook	Harvest Scene, Colorado/Green Overlook, Happy Canyon, North Trail, Maze Overlook

USGS TOPOGRAPHIC MAPS

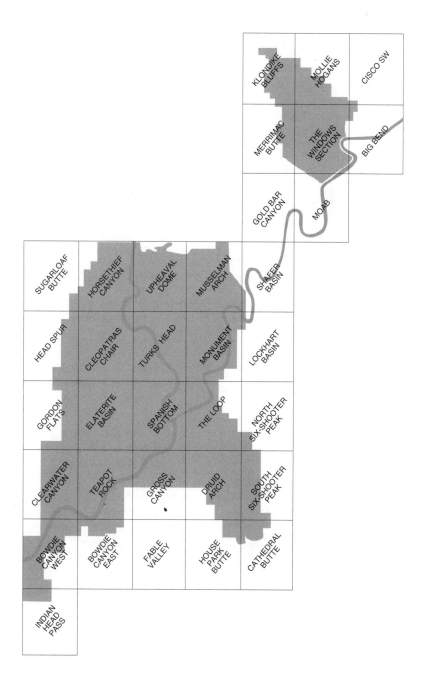

AUTHOR'S RECOMMENDATIONS

FOR PEOPLE WHO WANT A REALLY EASY DAY HIKE:

Arches	Sand Dune Arch
	Park Avenue
	Devils Garden (to Landscape Arch)
Island in the Sky	Mesa Arch
	Whale Rock
	White Rim Overlook
	Grand View
	Upheaval Dome Overlook
Needles	Pothole Point
	Cave Spring
Maze	Colorado/Green River Overlook (to Beehive Arch)

FOR PEOPLE WHO WANT AN EASY DAY HIKE, BUT NOT TOO EASY:

Arches	Broken Arch
	Tower Arch
Island in the Sky	Murphy Point
	Fort Bottom (access by four wheel drive)
Needles	Slickrock Foot Trail
	The Joint Trail
Maze	Granary

FOR PEOPLE WHO WANT A MODERATELY DIFFICULT HIKE, BUT NOT TOO DIFFICULT:

Arches	Devils Garden (to Double O Arch)
	Delicate Arch
	Fiery Furnace
Island in the Sky	Neck Spring
	Lathrop (to canyon rim)
	Moses (access by four wheel drive)
Needles	Squaw Canyon/Big Spring Canyon
	Chesler Park Loop
	Devils Pocket Loop
Maze	Great Gallery
	Maze Overlook
	Colorado/Green River Overlook
	Spanish Bottom

FOR PEOPLE WHO WANT A LONG, HARD DAY HIKE SO THEY CAN EAT ANYTHING THEY WANT FOR DINNER AND NOT FEEL GUILTY:

Arches	Devils Garden (primitive loop)
Island in the Sky	Syncline Dome Loop Murphy Basin Alcove Spring
Needles	Lost Canyon Squaw Canyon/Elephant Canyon Druid Arch Confluence Overlook Upper Salt Creek
Maze	Harvest Scene

FOR THAT FIRST NIGHT IN THE WILDERNESS:

Island in the Sky	Murphy Point Upheaval Canyon
Needles	Upper Salt Creek (out-and-back option) Squaw Canyon/Big Spring Canyon Elephant Hill to Squaw Canyon Chesler Park Loop
Maze	Happy Canyon Colorado/Green River Overlook

FOR PHOTOGRAPHERS:

Arches	Devils Garden Park Avenue Fiery Furnace Delicate Arch
Island in the Sky	Murphy Point Moses (access by four wheel drive) White Rim Overlook Grand View Point Overlook
Needles	The Joint Trail Peekaboo Lost Canyon Confluence Overlook Devils Pocket Loop
Maze	Maze Overlook Harvest Scene Colorado/Green River Overlook

FOR PEOPLE WHO WANT A MULTI-DAY BACKCOUNTRY ADVENTURE:

Island in the Sky	Alcove Spring/Syncline Loop
Needles	Big Needles Loop
	Chesler Park/Devils Kitchen
	Upper Salt Creek
Maze	Harvest Scene

FOR TRAIL RUNNERS AND POWER HIKERS:

Island in the Sky	Neck Spring
	Lathrop (to canyon rim)
	Upheaval Canyon
Needles	Squaw Canyon/Big Spring Canyon
	Squaw Canyon/Elephant Canyon

USING THIS GUIDEBOOK

This guidebook won't answer all the questions you have concerning your trip to Arches or Canyonlands national parks, but it should answer most of them. This book provides most of the basic information you need to plan a successful trip.

DISTANCES

In this guidebook, most distances came from odometer readings or from NPS signs and brochures. However, in some cases, estimates were made. Keep in mind that distance is often less important than difficulty. A rocky, 2-mile uphill trail can take longer and require more efort than 4 miles on a well-contoured trail on flat terrain. Often the trails and roads of these parks are better measured in hours instead of miles.

RATINGS

To help you plan your trip, each road description in this section includes vehicle recommendations. Vehicle ratings for backcountry roads came from experience in driving the roads and from NPS recommendations. These recommendations are, admittedly, on the conservative side. Play it safe, take a high-clearance four-wheel-drive to safely cover any road in the park. A high-clearance four-wheel-drive vehicle is required for all backcountry roads in the Needles and the Maze.

Difficulty ratings for trails serve as a general guide only, not the final word. What is difficult to one hiker may be easy to the next. In this guide-

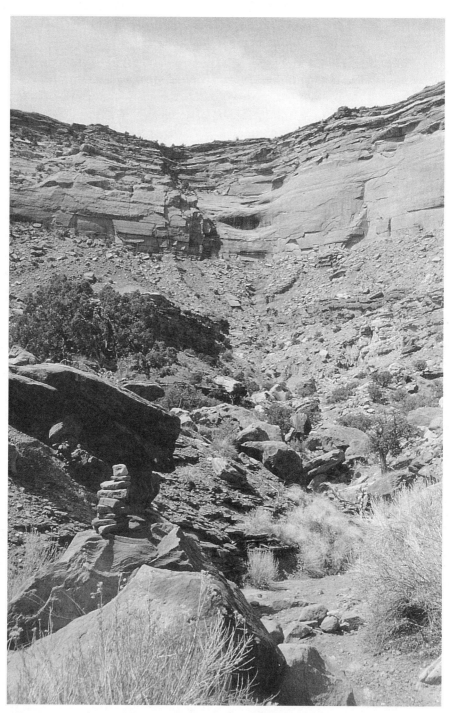

Many trails in Canyonlands National Park are rough and marked only with cairns, such as this section of the Gooseberry Trail in the Island in the Sky District.

book, difficulty ratings consider both how long and how strenuous the route is. Here are general definitions of the ratings:

Easy—Suitable for any hiker, including small children, without serious elevation gain, hazardous sections, or places where the trail is hard to follow.

Moderate—Suitable for hikers who have some experience and at least an average fitness level. Probably not suitable for small children. The hike may have some short sections where the trail is difficult to follow, and often includes some hills.

Difficult—Suitable for experienced hikers with above-average fitness level, often with sections of the trail that are difficult to follow or some off-trail sections that could require knowledge of route-finding with topo map and compass, sometimes with serious elevation gain, and possibly some hazardous conditions.

ELEVATION CHARTS

Many—but not all—hike descriptions include elevation charts. These charts are drawn at a small scale, so they can't give you a detailed picture of elevation gain and loss on a hike. However, they can give you a general idea of how much climbing or descending you face on that trail. Hikes without elevation charts are either very short hikes or hikes without significant elevation gain or loss.

TYPE OF TRIPS

Suggested hikes have been split into the following categories:

Loop—Starts and finishes at the same trailhead, with no (or very little) retracing of your steps.

Shuttle—A point-to-point trip that requires two vehicles (one left at the other end of the trail) or an arrangement where hikers are picked up at a designated time and place. The best way to manage the logistical problems of shuttles is to arrange for another party to start at the other end of the trail. When the two parties meet at a pre-determined point and then trade keys. When finished, they drive each other's vehicle home.

Out-and-Back—Traveling to a specific destination, then retracing your steps back to the trailhead.

MANAGING THE BACKCOUNTY

In January 1995, after extensive public input, the NPS published a new backcountry management plan for Canyonlands National Park. The new plan was needed because: visitation had quadrupled from 1984 (105,646 visitors) to 1993 (434,844) and this increased use posed many threats to the finite resources of the park. The plan established new regulations to preserve the fragile high desert environment.

In summary, the 1995 plan (which does not cover Arches National Park) made the following changes in the management of the backcountry of Canyonlands National Park:

- Established 19 backcountry zones for backpacking. Only 3—Island in the Sky/Syncline, Needles/Upper Salt Creek and Needles/Needles Trails—have designated campsites. The remaining zones allow at-large camping. Please refer to the color maps in the middle of the book and the chart on page 18.

- Limited the total number of backcountry permits to 63.

- Established a backcountry permit reservation system.

- Established a user fee to fund the backcountry reservation system and maintain backcountry facilities.

- Limited the length of backcountry stays to 7-10 days in any zone and established a limit of 14 consecutive days per trip.

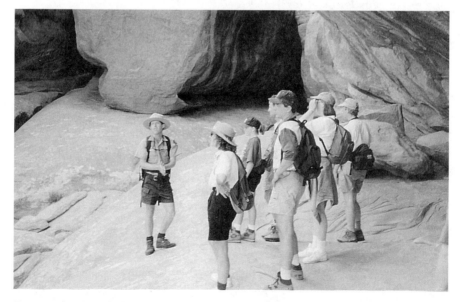

Rangers lead guided tours daily into the Fiery Furnace section of Arches National Park.

- Limited backpacking group size to 7 per party in the Needles and Island in the Sky districts and 5 per party in the Maze.
- Established vehicle group size at 10 for the Needles, 15 for the Island in the Sky and 9 for the Maze.
- Closed two sensitive areas to all entry.
- Prohibited all wood fires and wood gathering throughout the backcountry.
- Closed sections of some roads by converting them to hiking trails.
- Removed all garbage cans from the backcountry.
- Established acceptable noise levels.
- Prohibited all pets in the backcountry.
- Limited stock use (horses, mules, and burros) of the backcountry and prohibited llamas and goats.
- Required use of pelletized feed for stock 48 hours before and during any trip to the backcountry.
- Allowed caches under some circumstances.

SPECIAL REGULATIONS FOR BACKCOUNTRY USE

Canyonlands and Arches national parks have strict regulations to protect the fragile environment. Under these regulations, **you may not**

- Take pets, with or without a leash, into the backcountry.
- Drive vehicles off established roads.
- Collect, destroy, or deface any mineral, plant, wildlife, or natural feature.
- Take firearms, or any implement designed to discharge missiles, into the backcountry.
- Swim or bathe in any water source with the exception of the Colorado and Green rivers and along the Salt Creek backcountry road.
- Have a wood fire or gather wood.
- Go into the backcountry without an overnight permit. (Refer to page 18 for information on getting permits.)

AT-LARGE CAMPING

Most backpacking permits in the three districts of Canyonlands National Park (but not in Arches National Park) are for "at-large" campsites. This means you can camp anywhere subject to the following regulations. All at-large campsites must be:

- 300 feet from any water source, including seeps, potholes, springs, and streams, not including the Green and Colorado rivers.

- 300 feet from any archaeological site, including alcoves, rock art, surface scatters of lithics or ceramics, and partial or complete structures or ruins.

- At least 1 mile from a trailhead or road, including backcountry roads.

- Within the zone for which the permit is issued.

- In an area open to at-large camping.

- Left with the least possible evidence of use and environmental impact.

- Accessed by the least impacting route, using washes or rock surfaces to reach the campsite.

- Located on rock surfaces, previously disturbed sites, or surfaces without cryptobiotic soil crusts or vegetation.

WHAT IS AT-LARGE BACKPACKING?

In many areas in Canyonlands National Park—such as Lavender Canyon and Lower Salt Creek in the Needles, below the White Rim Road in Island in the Sky District and most of the Maze District—the NPS allows what is called "at-large" backpacking. All vehicle camping in these areas is restricted to designated backcountry camps, but backpackers can choose their own low-impact sites. However, you must follow all the regulations listed in this chapter and camp at least 1 mile from and out-of-sight of any road or trailhead.

This does not mean you can drive part way up a backcountry road, stop at a convenient point, then carry your pack a mile away from the road and spend the night. You must park your vehicle at a trailhead, not along the road.

The only place you can leave your vehicle overnight is at an official vehicle camp (if you have a permit for that site) or at a trailhead for either a road or a trail, with two exceptions— Peekaboo Camp and at the end of the Salt Creek Road in the Needles. For example, you can at-large backpack in Lavender Canyon or Salt Creek in the Needles, but you must leave your vehicle at the locked gate for these areas.

In Arches National Park, backpacking is allowed one-half mile from trails and one mile from roads with a few other restrictions.

HOW TO DRIVE

Of course you know how to drive, right? Driving some of the roads in Arches and Canyonlands might make you wonder. The most critical advice given out by the NPS is "don't be in a hurry." If you're on a tight schedule, you probably won't have much fun. You might wreck your vehicle, too, and the towing fee can bankrupt you.

Stay on the designated road and don't widen the road just to miss a mud puddle, small rock or a little ledge. If the road goes over a ledge, that's probably the best route and has been used by thousands of drivers who have gone before you. If each visitor widened the road a few inches, it would soon have a major negative impact on the fragile high desert environment.

Also, watch ahead for vehicles coming your way, especially in narrow sections or on switchbacks. If you see another vehicle coming, pull over at the first convenient spot. Don't assume the other driver has seen your vehicle or that there will be another good spot to pull off before the vehicles meet.

BACKPACKING PERMITS BY ZONE		
Area	Zone Name	Number of Permits
ISLAND IN THE SKY	Taylor Canyon	4
	Syncline	1*
	Upper West Basins	3
	Lower Basins	2
	Gooseberry/Lathrop	2
	Murphy Point	1
NEEDLES	Davis and Lavender	2
	Upper Salt Creek	4*
	Salt Creek/Horse Canyon	4
	Butler/West Side Canyons	2
	Red Lake/Grabens	5
	Needles North	1
MAZE	Maze Area	11
	Orange Cliffs	1
	High Spur	3

* = Designated backcountry campsites

HIKING THE HIGH DESERT

The Canyonlands are high desert country, so prepare yourself for this climate. That means having the right equipment and clothing, but it also means being mentally prepared.

For starters, you should make one major attitude adjustment. In most cases, the only water you'll ever drink in the desert is the water you carry with you. This differs significantly from most hiking areas where you can bank on filtering or purifying water from a stream or lake along the way. This is actually a difficult adjustment for people accustomed to hiking in non-desert climates, especially if it's their first time in the high desert. It won't be long, however, before the special character of the canyons creeps into your body and takes root, and then, you'll love the place, no matter how dry it is.

WHEN TO HIKE

In northern climates, most hiking occurs during the summer months, particularly July and August, but summer might be the worst time to go to the Canyonlands. Instead, choose one of the "shoulder seasons"—spring

Some trails simply follow the path of least resistance which is often a dry wash such as this section of the Gooseberry Trail in the Island in the Sky District. It might not be the shortest distance between two points, but it helps minimize damage to the cryptobiotic crust. An occasional cairn reminds hikers they're on the right route.

(March, April, or May) when the fabulous desert wildflowers bloom or in the fall (September, October, or November) when the weather is more pleasant. Also, spring and fall temperatures usually drop to a level to make hiking much more enjoyable than in summer months.

To get extra enjoyment out of hiking the high desert, take advantage of the early morning or late evening. The desert light is the purest early and late in the day when the temperature usually drops to a more tolerable level. Plus, you stand a better chance of seeing desert wildlife at these times. Some desert fauna is nocturnal, and even diurnal species often remain inactive during midday, but come out at dawn and dusk.

THE WATER DILEMMA

Hiking in the high desert is, simply put, more exercise than hiking in moist climates. You really can't go lightweight because you need to carry your water. Experts recommend taking 1 gallon of water per person per day for long day hikes and even more for backpacking. For many people, this essentially limits the length of your trip to two or three nights. A gallon of water weighs about 8 pounds. That means, for example, that a four-person group on a three-day trip (two nights out) would have to carry a total of 96 pounds of water.

If you're planning a longer trip and the weight of your pack is stretching your physical abilities, cut out weight in other ways instead of reducing water supply. For example, abandon optional equipment like extra camera gear or clothes—or at least invest in lightweight gear. It won't kill you to wear the same underwear two days in a row, but running short on water can kill you.

It might be tempting to leave your tent home to save weight, but a tent can be a lifesaver if bad weather blows in. However, you can take a lightweight, three-season tent or a four-person group can substitute a lightweight four-person tent instead of carrying two smaller tents that, together, weigh more.

Food presents a special challenge. The lightest food (pre-prepared, freeze-dried meals or dehydrated foods like pasta, rice and oatmeal) take water to prepare. This means you have to use precious water for cooking.

This might seem like heresy to backpacking gourmands, but one alternative is to take the no-cooking option. Prepare evening meals in advance in leak-proof containers or make sandwiches. Plan on snacking for breakfast and lunch. This might seem radical, but you can save weight in two ways—you use less water and need less gas for your stove. You could, actually, leave your stove and gas at home if you're sure of the weather forecast and have no chance of running into cold weather.

THE DESERT SUN

Although the lack of water presents the biggest challenge for the hiker, the abundance of sunshine also requires special preparation and planning. Three pieces of equipment that might be optional elsewhere—a wide-brimmed hat, sunglasses, and sunscreen—are essential for desert hiking.

Don't underestimate the power of the desert sun. You might think you have a tan and don't need sunscreen, but you're almost always wrong. If you're still lily white from your winter hibernation, start hiking with sunscreen protection rated at 25-30. Later, if you want a tan, move down to 8-12. If you expose your skin without sunscreen, do it only for a hour or so per day. You'll be unpleasantly shocked by how fast you can burn, and a bad sunburn, besides being unhealthy can ruin your vacation.

Also, pay attention to the type of clothing you wear. When picking your wardrobe, generally go "light and white," and try for natural fibers like cotton whenever possible. A round, wide-brimmed hat keeps more sun off your neck and ears than a baseball-type hat, and be sure to get one with a drawstring. If the wind keeps blowing off your hat, you might not wear it, and get fried by the desert sun. Also, that old stand-by, the bandanna, can be draped from the back of your hat to prevent you from becoming a "redneck." Long pants and long-sleeved shirts cut down the amount of skin exposed to the sun.

The sun isn't the only reason to wear long pants. If you're going cross-country or on a rough trail, you definitely should wear long pants. If you don't, the desert flora (most species armed with spines) will constantly take

Hiking down the Hogback Trail on Murphy Basin Loop in the Island in the Sky District.

little nicks out of your legs. Such wounds will heal, of course, but wearing long pants will be less painful, and you can avoid being a poster child for Neosporin.

Another piece of equipment essential for enjoying the desert is good footwear. You don't need the extra-heavy boots mountain climbers wear, but you need sturdy boots of at least ankle height. Running or cross-training shoes might suffice for easier trips on well-defined trails, but anything long and rough calls for sturdier boots, even more so than in forested hiking areas in temperate zone mountain ranges.

FAINT TRAILS

Most of the short, frequently used trails in both Arches and Canyonlands national parks are well-defined and marked, and nobody has problems following them. However, some trails receive infrequent use and can be difficult to find in places. Plus, terrain such as slickrock and canyon washes makes construction and maintenance of permanent trails difficult.

If you get in a situation where you can't see the trail, don't panic. Usually you can look ahead to see where the trail goes. Even if you can't, don't worry about being off the trail for a short distance. Some trails simply follow canyon washes with an occasional cairn to remind you that you're still on the correct route. In a narrow canyon, the trail can rarely go anywhere but between the canyon walls. However, if you've gone a long way without seeing a cairn, you might be in the wrong canyon and need to backtrack to the last cairn. Again, don't panic. Get out the topo map and figure out where

Many trails simply follow the canyon wash.

you went wrong—or better yet, keep it out as you go along, so you'll know your exact location at all times.

Most trails in these parks are marked with cairns, but cairns can be knocked down or blown away. Also, hikers have been known to put up "unofficial" cairns to mark a route back to their camp or favorite hiking area.

SHARING

Each of us want our own private wilderness area, but that only happens in our dreams. Lots of people use the national parks. To give everybody an equal chance of having a great experience, we all must work at politely sharing the wilderness. In some places in the Canyonlands, for example, hikers, mountain bikers, and four-wheelers share the same backcountry road. Every situation is different, but safety and courtesy should always dictate the decision on who yields. In most cases, hikers should yield to mountain bikers or vehicles, and mountain bikers should yield to vehicles.

In other cases, hikers share trails with backcountry horsemen (although stock use is infrequent at Canyonlands and Arches because of the dry climate). Both hikers and backcountry horsemen have every right to be on the trail. Keep in mind that horses and other stock animals are much less maneuverable than hikers, so it becomes the hiker's responsibility to yield the right-of-way. Hike uphill from the trail about 20 feet and stand quietly while stock passes.

Another instance requiring the polite sharing of wilderness is choosing your campsite. If you get to a popular at-large camping area late in the day and all good campsites are taken, don't crowd another camper. This is most aggravating. These sites rightfully go on a first-come, first-served basis. If you're late, you have the responsibility to move on or take a less desirable site a respectable distance away from other campers. In some backcountry zones, designated campsites have multiple tentsites. Try to pick one as far away from other campers as possible.

ZERO IMPACT

Going into a national park such as Yellowstone is like visiting a famous museum. You obviously do not want to leave your mark on an art treasure in the museum. If everybody going through the museum left one little mark, the piece of art would be quickly destroyed—and of what value is a big building full of trashed art? The same goes for a pristine wilderness such as Canyonlands and Arches national parks, which are as magnificent as any masterpiece by any artist. If we all left just one little mark on the landscape, the wilderness would soon be despoiled.

A wilderness can accommodate a reasonable amount of human use as long as everybody behaves. But a few thoughtless or uninformed visitors can ruin it for everybody who follows. And need for good manners applies to all wilderness users, not just backpackers. Day hikers should also strictly adhere to the "zero-impact" principles. We all must leave no clues that we have gone before.

Most of us know better than to litter—in or out of the wilderness. Be sure you leave nothing, regardless of how small it is, along the trail or at the campsite. This means you should pack out everything, including orange peels, flip tops, cigarette butts, and gum wrappers. Also, pick up any trash that others leave behind.

Follow the main trail. Avoid cutting switchbacks and walking on vegetation beside the trail. In the desert, some terrain is very fragile so, if possible, stay on the trail. If you're hiking off trail, try to hike on slickrock or in canyon washes.

Don't pick up "souvenirs," such as rocks, antlers or wildflowers. The next person wants to see them, too, and collecting such souvenirs violates park regulations.

Hikers leaving Upper Elephant Canyon and heading west into Cyclone Canyon on Confluence Overlook Trail in the Needles District. In the background, note a sea of cheatgrass, an introduced species that "cheats" native species of water and soil nutrients.

Avoid making loud noises that may disturb others. Remember, sound travels easily to the other side of the canyon. Be courteous.

Bury human waste 6-8 inches deep and pack out used toilet paper. This is a good reason to carry a lightweight trowel. Keep wastes at least 300 feet away from any water source.

Finally, and perhaps most importantly, strictly follow the pack-in/pack-out rule. If you carry something into the backcountry, consume it or carry it out.

Zero impact—and put your ear to the ground in the wilderness and listen carefully. Thousands of people coming behind you are thanking you for your courtesy and good sense.

ENDANGERED DIRT

Some advocates of zero-impact recreation suggest "leave only footprints," but in the high desert, this is bad advice. One footprint can destroy decades of growth.

Crypotobiotic crust is the foundation of life in the high desert. It provides a seedbed for the desert plant community and serves as a sponge, retaining the precious moisture of a dry climate. The crust is also the primary source for fixation of nitrogen which is critically to all life in the desert. This crust is a complex community of microorganisms, the most important of which are called cyanobacteria.

When mature, cryptobiotic soil has a lumpy, black-tinged crust. In earlier stages, the crust is almost invisible. If you step on it, ride on it or drive on it, it blows away and erodes, and then, it takes many years, if not decades, to recover.

This is a prime reason to stay on trails and roads. If you have to hike off-trail, try to stay on slickrock or in canyon washes to prevent stepping on cryptobiotic crust. Usually when somebody says "watch your step," they have safety in mind, but in the Canyonlands, this can mean the preservation of the high desert environment.

MAKE IT A SAFE TRIP

The Scouts have been guided for decades by what is perhaps the best single piece of safety advice—Be Prepared! For starters, this means carrying survival and first-aid materials, proper clothing, compass, and topographic map—and knowing how to use them.

Perhaps the second-best piece of safety advice is to tell somebody where you're going and when you plan to return. Pilots must file flight plans before every trip, and anybody venturing into a blank spot on the map should do the same. File your "flight plan" with a friend or relative before taking off.

Close behind your flight plan and being prepared with proper equipment is physical conditioning. Being fit not only makes wilderness travel more fun, it makes it safer. To whet your appetite for more knowledge of wilderness safety and preparedness, here are a few more tips.

- Check the weather forecast. Be careful not to get caught at high altitude by a bad storm or in a narrow canyon by a flash flood. Watch cloud formations closely, so you don't get stranded on a ridgeline during a lightning storm. Avoid traveling during prolonged periods of cold weather.

- Avoid traveling alone in the wilderness.

- Keep your party together.

In several places in both parks the National Park Service has installed ladders to help hikers get over dangerous spots, such as this spot on the trail between Big Spring Canyon and Elephant Canyon in the Needles District.

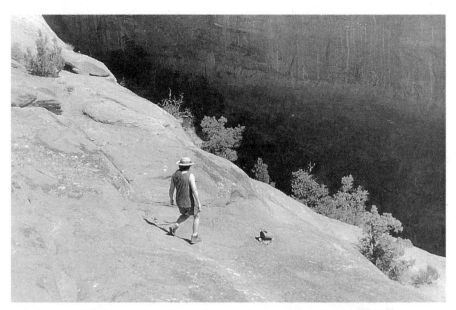

Many trails in both parks follow cairns over expanses of solid slickrock.

- Know the preventive measures, symptoms, and treatment of hypothermia, the silent killer.
- Study basic survival and first aid before leaving home.
- Don't eat wild plants.
- Before you leave for the trailhead, find out as much as you can about the route, especially the potential hazards.
- Don't exhaust yourself or other members of your party by traveling too far or too fast. Let the slowest person set the pace.
- Don't wait until you're confused to look at your maps. Follow them as you go along, from the moment you start moving up the trail, so you have a continual fix on your location.
- If you get lost, don't panic. Sit down and relax for a few minutes while you carefully check your topo map and take a reading with your compass. Confidently plan your next move. It's often smart to retrace your steps until you find familiar ground, even if you think it might lengthen your trip. Lots of people get temporarily lost in the wilderness and survive—usually by calmly and rationally dealing with the situation.
- Stay clear of all wild animals. Never feed wild animals.
- Take a first-aid kit that includes, at a minimum, the following items: Sewing needle, snake-bite kit, aspirin, antibacterial ointment, two antiseptic swabs, two butterfly bandages, adhesive tape, four adhesive strips, four gauze pads, two triangular bandages, codeine

tablets, two inflatable splints, moleskin, one roll 3-inch gauze, CPR shield, rubber gloves, and lightweight first-aid instructions.

- Take a survival kit that includes, at a minimum, the following items: Compass, whistle, matches in a waterproof container, cigarette lighter, candle, signal mirror, fire starter, aluminum foil, water purification tablets, space blanket, and flare.

Last but not least, don't forget that the best defense against unexpected hazards is knowledge. Read up on the latest in wilderness safety information in the recently published Wild Country Companion. Check the back of this guidebook for ordering information.

YOU MIGHT NEVER KNOW WHAT HIT YOU

The high desert environs of the Canyonlands are prone to sudden thunderstorms, especially in spring and summer months. If you get caught by a lightning storm, take special precautions. Remember:

- *Lightning can travel far ahead of the storm, so be sure to take cover before the storm hits.*

- *Don't try to make it back to your vehicle. Instead, seek shelter even if it's only a short way back to the trailhead. It isn't worth the risk. Lightning storms usually don't last long, and from a safe vantage point, you might enjoy the sights and sounds.*

- *Be especially careful not to get caught on a mountaintop or exposed ridge; under large, solitary trees; in the open; or near standing water.*

- *Seek shelter in a low-lying area, ideally in a dense stand of small, uniformly sized trees.*

- *Stay away from anything that might attract lightning, such as metal tent poles, graphite fishing rods, or pack frames.*

- *Get in a crouch position and place both feet firmly on the ground.*

- *If you have a pack (without a metal frame) or a sleeping pad with you, put your feet on it for extra insulation against shock.*

- *Don't huddle together. Instead, sit 50 feet apart, so if somebody gets hit by lightning, others in your party can give first aid.*

- *If you're in a tent, stay there, in your sleeping bag with your feet on your sleeping pad.*

THE SILENT KILLER

Be aware of the danger of hypothermia—a condition in which the body's internal temperature drops below normal. It can lead to mental and physical collapse and death.

Hypothermia is caused by exposure to cold, and is aggravated by wetness, wind, and exhaustion. The moment you begin to lose heat faster than your body produces it, you're suffering from exposure. Your body starts involuntary exercise such as shivering to stay warm and makes involuntary adjustments to preserve normal temperature in vital organs, restricting bloodflow in the extremities. Both responses drain your energy reserves. The only way to stop the drain is to reduce the degree of exposure.

With full-blown hypothermia, as energy reserves are exhausted, cold reaches the brain, depriving you of good judgment and reasoning power. You won't be aware that this is happening. You lose control of your hands. Your internal temperature slides downward. Without treatment, this slide leads to stupor, collapse, and death.

To defend against hypothermia, stay dry. When clothes get wet, they lose about 90 percent of their insulating value. Wool loses relatively less heat; cotton, down, and some synthetics lose more. Choose rain clothes that cover the head, neck, body, and legs, and provide good protection against wind-driven rain. Most hypothermia cases develop in air temperatures between 30 and 50 degrees Fahrenheit, but hypothermia can develop in warmer temperatures.

If your party is exposed to wind, cold, and wet, think hypothermia. Watch yourself and others for these symptoms: uncontrollable fits of shivering; vague, slow, slurred speech; memory lapses; incoherence; immobile, fumbling hands; frequent stumbling or a lurching gait; drowsiness (to sleep is to die); apparent exhaustion; and inability to get up after a rest. When a member of your party has hypothermia, he or she may deny any problem. Believe the symptoms, not the victim.

Even mild symptoms demand treatment, as follows:

• Get the victim out of the wind and rain.

• Strip off all wet clothes.

• If the victim is only mildly impaired, give him or her warm drinks. Then get the victim in warm clothes and a warm sleeping bag. Place well-wrapped water bottles filled with heated water close to the victim.

• If the victim is badly impaired, attempt to keep him or her awake. Put the victim in a sleeping bag with another person—both naked. If you have a double bag, put two warm people in with the victim.

MOAB MONTHLY CLIMATOLOGICAL DATA

MONTH	AVG. HIGH TEMP	AVG. LOW TEMP	MAX. HIGH TEMP	MAX. LOW TEMP	# DAYS OVER 90°F	# DAYS UNDER 32°F	AVG. PRECIP (INCHES)	% OF ANNUAL PRECIP.
Jan.	43.9°	18.8°	67°	1°	0	30	0.5"	5%
Feb.	52.7°	25.1°	75°	1°	0	23	0.5"	5%
March	63.9°	33.3°	86°	19°	0	15	0.9"	9%
April	76.6°	38.9°	92°	26°	2	3	1.2"	12%
May	84.3°	49.4°	97°	34°	10	0	1.1"	11%
June	97.6°	57.9°	108°	38°	28	0	0.1"	1%
July	99.5°	61.9°	109°	50°	29	0	1.2"	12%
Aug	98.6°	61.5°	107°	49°	30	0	0.8"	7%
Sept.	86.1°	50.4°	102°	30°	12	1	0.8"	7%
Oct.	77.1°	40.3°	92°	26°	4	2	1.6"	15%
Nov.	58.4°	31.7°	78°	16°	0	17	1.2"	12%
Dec.	47.9°	21.4°	60°	10°	0	29	0.5"	4%

Temperatures are given in Fahrenheit degrees. To convert to Celsius, subtract 32 from the Fahrenheit number, then multiply by 5/9 or .55.

Precipitation is given in inches. To convert to centimeters, multiply inches by 2.54.

Data from Atlas Minerals Weather Station, Moab, Utah from 1980 through 1990.

This chart is for an elevation of 4,000 feet. Most of Canyonlands is at a higher elevation and hence will be cooler in both summer and winter.

Supplied courtesy of William Baron, Curator, Historical Climate Records Office, Northern Arizona University, Flagstaff, Arizona (1991).

CHECKLISTS

HIKING

Equipment for Day Hiking

❏ Your FALCONGUIDE
❏ Day pack or fanny pack
❏ Water bottles
❏ First-aid kit
❏ Survival kit
❏ Compass
❏ Maps
❏ Pocket knife

❏ Toilet trowel
❏ Toilet paper
❏ Sunscreen and lip lotion
❏ Sunglasses
❏ Binoculars
❏ Camera and extra film
❏ Flashlight and extra batteries

Added Equipment for Overnight Trips

❏ Tent and waterproof fly
❏ Sleeping bag (20 degrees F
    or warmer) and stuff sack
❏ Sleeping pad
❏ Cooking pots and pot holder
❏ More water bottles
❏ Full-size backpack
❏ Cup, bowl, and eating utensils

❏ Garbage sacks
❏ Zip-locked bags
❏ Paper towels
❏ Nylon cord (50 ft.)
❏ Small towel
❏ Personal toilet kit
❏ Notebook and pencil
❏ Lightweight camp stove
    and adequate fuel

CLOTHING: In general, strive for natural fibers such as cotton and wool and "earth tones" instead of bright colors. Dig around in the closet for something "dull." Your wilderness partners will appreciate it. Try out the clothing before leaving home to make sure everything fits loosely with no chafing. In particular, make sure your boots are broken in, lest they break you on the first day of the hike.

Clothing for Day Hiking

❏ Large-brimmed hat or cap
❏ Sturdy hiking boots
❏ Light, natural fiber socks
❏ Lightweight, light-colored
    hiking shorts or long pants

❏ Light colored, long-sleeve shirt
❏ Lightweight, windproof coat
❏ Raingear
❏ Mittens or gloves

Additional Clothing for Overnight Trips

❏ Warm hat (i.e. stocking cap)
❏ Long underwear
❏ Water-resistant, windproof jacket
❏ Sweater and/or insulated vest
❏ Long pants
❏ Underwear

❏ One pair of socks for each day,
    plus one extra pair
❏ Mittens or gloves
❏ Extra shirts
❏ Sandals or lightweight shoes
    for wearing in camp

FOOD: For day hiking, bring high-energy snacks for lunching along the way. For overnight trips, bring enough food, including high-energy snacks, but don't overburden yourself with too much food. Plan meals carefully, bringing just enough food, plus some emergency rations. Freeze-dried foods are the lightest and safest, but expensive and not really necessary. Don't forget hot and cold drinks. Try to minimize food that requires extra water to prepare.

MOUNTAIN BIKING

Equipment for Day Trips

- First-aid kit, including aspirin
- Duct tape (a small roll)
- Basic tool kit and spare parts
- Tire changing tools
- Extra tubes (two or more depending on length and difficulty)
- Patch kit (especially if you don't bring two tubes)
- Tire pump
- Map
- Compass
- Helmet
- Sunglasses
- Sunscreen
- Pocket knife
- Head lamp with extra batteries
- Parachute cord
- Waterproof matches or lighter (or both)
- Toilet paper and trowel
- Notepad and pencil
- Adequate water
- Emergency food

Additional Equipment for Overnight Trips (without Support Vehicle)

- Tent
- Sleeping bag
- Ground pad
- Stove and extra fuel
- Cooking pot and gripper
- Cup & eating utensils
- Garbage bags
- Book
- Eating utensils
- Water filter (recommended by NPS) or purification tablets
- Towel and biodegradable soap
- Personal toiletries
- Cleaning pad
- Camping permit

CLOTHING: Although quality cycling gear can be expensive, it's usually worth it. For example, well-designed cycling shorts will be worth their weight in gold on the day you wore the low-priced version and started chafing badly. The same goes for jerseys, tights, and coats. Take a test ride with new clothing before taking a long desert trip with it.

Clothing for Day Trips

- Padded cycling shorts
- Long-sleeve shirt
- Long pants or tights
- Lightweight rain jacket
- Cycling jersey
- Cycling shoes
- Cycling gloves
- Rain pants

Extra Clothing for Overnight Trips

❐ Change of clothes
❐ Insulated underwear
❐ Stocking cap
❐ Waterproof shoe covers

❐ Warm gloves or mittens
❐ Sandals
❐ Waterproof mittens or overgloves
❐ Gore-tex socks

FOOD: For day trips, bring lots of high-energy snacks. For overnight trips, bring enough food, including high-energy snacks, but don't overburden yourself with too much food. Plan meals carefully, bringing just enough food, plus some emergency rations. Freeze-dried foods are the lightest and safest. Don't forget hot and cold drinks. Try to minimize food that requires extra water to prepare.

FOUR-WHEELING

❐ Map
❐ Compass
❐ Full gas tank
❐ Extra gas in multiple containers
❐ Good tires
❐ Tire sealant
❐ Air pump
❐ Small board to support
  jack on sand
❐ Spare fuses
❐ Basic tools
❐ Repair manual for your vehicle
❐ Water in multiple containers
❐ Water filter
❐ Insect repellent
❐ Sun screen
❐ Emergency food
❐ Matches
❐ Guidebooks for local area

❐ Duct tape
❐ Spray lubricant/cleaner
❐ Litter bag
❐ Saw or ax
❐ First aid kit
❐ Roadside emergency reflectors
❐ Cellular phone
  (for emergency calls)
❐ Sleeping bag and warm clothing
❐ Extra eyeglasses
❐ Sunglasses
❐ Extra car keys (accessible
  when vehicle locked)
❐ Flashlight and extra batteries
❐ Tow rope
❐ Jumper cables
❐ Toilet paper and small shovel
❐ Binoculars
❐ Camping permit (for
  overnight trips)

ARCHES NATIONAL PARK

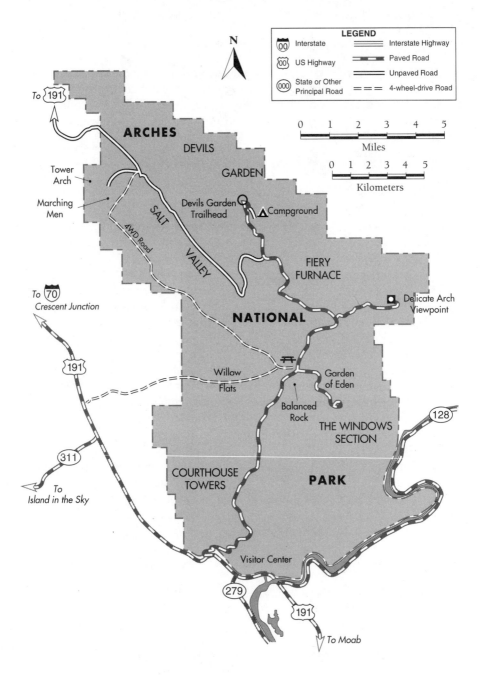

ARCHES NATIONAL PARK

OVERVIEW

Compared to many national parks, Arches is small (73,379 acres), but it's also very scenic and very popular. Moab, Utah, a small tourist hub just south of Arches, provides all services.

Arches was designated a national monument in 1929 and then expanded and designated a national park in 1971. The park is open 24 hours a day, 7 days a week, and the visitor center is open every day except Christmas. It's open from 8:00 a.m. to 4:30 p.m., from September to mid-April and later during summer months. The park has a 52-site campground at Devils Garden, but places go on a first-come, first-served basis and getting a spot can be difficult.

In Arches National Park, water, extreme temperatures, and other geologic forces have created the greatest diversity of arches in the world, along with many other multi-hued, finely sculpted rock formations. Delicate Arch, perhaps the park's most famous feature, shows up in an endless array of videos, postcards, posters, books and magazines. However, the numerous arches along the Devils Garden hike, the cathedralistic columns of the Park Avenue, the cavern-like canyons of Fiery Furnace, along with many other spectacular features rival the Delicate Arch (and just about everything else in nature!) for awesome beauty.

A hole in a rock has to have an opening of at least 3 feet to be officially listed as an arch and be given a name. Arches National Park has more than 2,400 arches, a preponderance of arches that makes Arches National Park unique on earth. In fact, there is no place even remotely like it.

Arches is not for the serious hiker. Instead, it's nicely suited for the visitor who doesn't mind seeing most scenery from the car window or on short walks. The trails offer spectacular scenery, but with one exception, they are all short day hikes. And, unlike Canyonlands National Park, Arches offers limited opportunities to the four-wheeler, with only three short backcountry road sections.

GETTING THERE

Arches National Park is located 25 miles south of Interstate 70 or 5 miles north of Moab on U.S. Highway 191. The starting points for hikes and drives are referenced from the entrance station.

Type of trail:	Loop.
Type of trip:	Short day hike.
Total distance:	0.2 mile.
Elevation change:	Minimal.
Time required:	15-30 minutes.
Maps:	Trails Illustrated Arches National Park and USGS Arches National Park.
Difficulty:	Easy.
Starting point:	Arches Visitor Center.

The hike: This is a very short (less than 0.25 mile) interpretive trail starting and ending at the Arches Visitor Center. Numbered signs along the way (which correspond with a booklet available at the trailhead) identify and explain the characteristics of the surrounding desert and ecology. Even if you're physically able to do longer hikes and plan to do so later in the day, you might want to take this trail first—just to get a good base of knowledge about desert plants that you can then try to find on your other hikes.

DESERT NATURE TRAIL, PARK AVENUE

© National Geographic/Trails Illustrated

2 PARK AVENUE

See Map on facing page

Type of trail:	Shuttle.
Type of trip:	Short day hike.
Total distance:	1 mile.
Elevation change:	320 feet.
Time required:	30-60 minutes.
Maps:	Trails Illustrated Arches National Park and USGS Arches National Park.
Difficulty:	Easy.
Starting point:	Park Avenue Parking Area (on your left 2.5 miles from the entrance station) or Courthouse Towers Parking Area (on your right 3.7 miles from the entrance station) in the shadow of massive Courthouse Towers.

The hike: The Park Avenue Trail is most aptly named for New York City's famous street. Early travelers noticed a similarity between these sandstone spires and the famous skyscrapers along New York's Park Avenue, and the name stuck. The main difference, of course, is that the "skyscrapers" of Arches National Park were sculpted by nature.

Although you can start at either end of this shuttle trail, starting at the south end results in a totally downhill hike. However, if you want to take this shuttle route as you leave the park, start at the north end, and have somebody pick you up at the south end. If you can't arrange a shuttle, this

Park Avenue in Arches National Park is more awe-inspiring than the famous street in New York City.

hike is definitely still worth taking, even with double the mileage (still only 2 miles) by going out and back.

You'll really be missing something if you leave Arches without taking this short hike. You can see the Courthouse Towers, Tower of Babel, Three Gossips, Organ, and other grand "skyscrapers" from the road, but if you don't take this hike, you'll miss the truly stimulating experience of walking among them.

The trail starts out as a concrete path leading to a scenic overlook about 100 yards from the trailhead. From here, a well-defined trail goes through juniper and cactus until it melts into a slickrock dry wash and stays there until just before you return to the main road. The trail disappears, but there's no chance of getting lost. Stay in the dry wash and follow well-placed cairns to the Courthouse Towers Parking Area.

3 BALANCED ROCK

Type of trail:	Loop.
Type of trip:	Short day hike.
Total distance:	0.2 mile.
Time required:	15-30 minutes.
Maps:	Trails Illustrated Arches National Park and USGS Arches National Park.
Difficulty:	Easy.
Starting point:	Balanced Rock Parking Area on the east side of the main park road 9 miles from the entrance station.

The hike: This is a very short hike, but it's perfect for travelers who would like to stretch their legs without working up a sweat. You can see Balanced Rock and read about it on an interpretive display from near the paved road, but it's not the same as getting up close. The trail makes a short loop around Balanced Rock and returns to the parking area.

The forces of nature sculpted Balanced Rock out of Entrada Sandstone. Technically, this is called a "caprock" of harder Slick Rock Member (a type of Entrada Sandstone) perched on a pedestal of softer Dewey Bridge Member (also Entrada Sandstone). The pedestal erodes more quickly than the more resistant caprock. The entire Balanced Rock formation is 128 feet high, and the rock itself measures 55 feet.

Balanced Rock used to have a companion called, of course, "Chip-Off-the-Old-Block," but it toppled during the winter of 1975-1976. You can still see its pedestal on the south side of Balanced Rock.

BALANCED ROCK, WINDOWS PRIMITIVE LOOP, DOUBLE ARCH

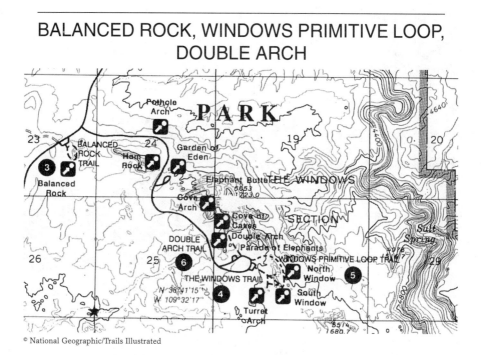

© National Geographic/Trails Illustrated

---

4 WINDOWS PRIMITIVE LOOP

Type of trail:	Out-and-back or loop.
Type of trip:	Short day hike.
Total distance:	0.9 mile for out and back, 1.25 miles for loop, plus short side trips.
Elevation change:	Minimal.
Time required:	30-60 minutes.
Maps:	Trails Illustrated Arches National Park and USGS Arches National Park.
Difficulty:	Easy.
Starting point:	Windows Parking Area.

Finding the trailhead: To find the trailhead, drive 9.2 miles north into the park on the main road until it forks. Take a right (east) and drive 3 miles to the Windows Parking Area.

The hike: The scenery is sensational on this short hike, but don't expect to have it to yourself. Almost everybody who comes to the park hikes up to see these spectacular arches. When you hear somebody talking about over-crowding in the national parks, the Windows section of Arches often comes to mind. Therefore, consider taking this short hike early or late in the day when the crowds will be somewhat diminished and when you are more likely to find a place to park.

The Windows.

Even though it seems like it should be the other way around, the trail heads to the North Window and then to the South Window. On the way to the North Window, you should take a short side trip to the right (south) to see Turret Arch. The Windows are sometimes called "The Spectacles," and you can see why. If you hike the primitive loop around the back of the arches, you can see the "nose" on which the spectacles rest.

It's fairly easy to go off-trail and climb up right under North Window and Turret Arch. Do not attempt to climb into South Window. Several people have fallen while trying or have gotten stranded here. Be careful not to fall or to damage any vegetation or natural features. Also, hang onto your hat. The strong winds in the area tend to blow it off as soon as you reach either arch.

After you finish marveling at the Windows and Turret Arch, you can retrace your steps back to the parking lot (about 0.9 mile total distance) or you can turn this into a longer walk (about 1.25 miles total distance) by taking the Windows Primitive Loop Trail. The well-defined loop trail starts from the viewpoint of South Window. It makes a small circle around the Windows, giving you another great view of North Window. It also offers a glimpse at the native vegetation of the area. The primitive loop trail hits the parking lot about 50 yards north of the main trailhead.

5 DOUBLE ARCH

		See Map on Page 39
Type of trail:	Out-and-back.	
Type of trip:	Short day hike.	
Total distance:	0.5 mile.	
Elevation change:	Minimal.	
Time required:	15-30 minutes.	
Maps:	Trails Illustrated Arches National Park and USGS Arches National Park.	
Difficulty:	Easy.	
Starting point:	Double Arch Parking Area.	

Finding the trailhead: To find the trailhead, drive 9.2 miles north into the park on the main road until it forks. Take the right fork for 3 miles to the

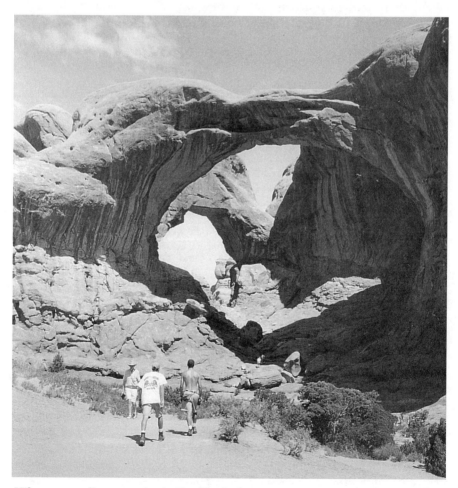

Hikers marveling at majestic Double Arch.

Windows Parking Area and keep going around a loop in the parking area for about a quarter mile and park in the Double Arch Parking Area on your right (north).

The hike: The short (about 0.25 mile one way), relatively flat hike to Double Arch goes through scattered junipers and oaks. In the spring, you might see Utah's state flower, the sego lily, a large, single, cream-colored flower. The trail is well defined and easy to follow all the way. Along the way, off to your left, you can see the series of buttes called the Parade of Elephants.

Double Arch looks sort of average from the parking area, but as you approach, its massiveness starts to sink in. Then, when you get there (and especially if you can climb up right under the arches), the imposing size of the arch becomes absolutely clear. It's the third largest arch opening in the park.

You can lengthen your trip by climbing up under Double Arch, but be careful not to disturb vegetation or natural features. If each person visiting this area left only a tiny mark, it wouldn't take long for the impact to be devastating.

6 DELICATE ARCH

Type of trail:	Out-and-back.
Type of trip:	Day hike.
Total distance:	3 miles.
Elevation change:	480 feet.
Time required:	2-3 hours.
Maps:	Trails Illustrated Arches National Park and USGS Arches National Park.
Difficulty:	Moderate.
Starting point:	Wolfe Ranch Parking Area.

Finding the trailhead: To find the trailhead, drive 11.7 miles north into the park on the main road until you see the right-hand turn to Delicate Arch and Wolfe Ranch. Turn right and drive another 1.2 miles to the parking area on your left (north). A lot for oversize vehicles in on your right.

The hike: If you've ever seen a postcard or poster of Arches National Park, you've probably seen Delicate Arch. This amazing arch has become the symbol of Arches National Park, which is somewhat surprising since it's barely visible from the road.

You have two options for viewing this magnificent natural feature. You can take a 1.5 mile trail (3 miles round trip) which goes right under the arch or you can go to the Delicate Arch Viewpoint or take a 5-minute walk to a

Hikers on the ledge leaving Delicate Arch.

closer viewpoint. If you choose the hiking option, be aware that the trail to Delicate Arch is not a stroll. This is a real hike, and you should be prepared. Bring extra water (a minimum of 1 quart per person), wear good hiking shoes, and try to avoid the midday heat. There is little shade along this trail. The NPS describes the trail as "moderately strenuous."

At the trailhead you can see the remains of the Wolfe Ranch, settled in 1888 and abandoned in 1910. Shortly after leaving the trailhead, you cross over Salt Wash on a bridge. Right after the bridge, you might notice a large pile of "green stuff" on your right. This is volcanic ash with a high iron

DELICATE ARCH

content that has gone through a chemical process that gives it this greenish cast. Just after the bridge, you can take a short side trip to the left to a Ute petroglyph panel. During the first part of the hike, watch for collared lizards. These large lizards can run on their hind feet when chasing prey.

For the first half-mile or so, you hike on a wide, well-defined, mostly level trail. Then, the excellent trail disappears, and you start a gradual ascent to Delicate Arch. Most of the rest of the trip is on slickrock, so be alert. You have to follow cairns the rest of the way, and sometimes the "cairns" are only one rock. As you get closer to Delicate Arch, you can see Frame Arch off to your right. This arch forms a perfect "frame" for a photograph of Delicate Arch. If you decide to climb up this short, steep slope to get that photograph, be careful.

Just before you get to Delicate Arch, the trail goes along a ledge for about 200 yards. This section of trail was blasted out of the cliff, and you can still see the bore holes in the rock. If you have children with you, watch them carefully in this section. Just after the ledge ends, you see Delicate Arch with its huge opening (33 feet wide and 45 feet high). You can take an awe-inspiring walk down to right below the arch, but you might ruin somebody's photo. A shot of Delicate Arch with the often snowcapped La Sal Mountains as a backdrop must be one of those photos every professional photographer has to have in his or her file, so one or two shutterbugs are usually setting up tripods for the grand view.

If you prefer the less strenuous option for seeing Delicate Arch, drive past the Wolfe Ranch Parking Area and go another 1.2 miles. From the parking area, take one of two short walks—a short (0.5 mile) trail to the top of a

Delicate Arch, the symbol of Arches National Park.

small ridge where you can look north for a good view of Delicate Arch, or an even shorter trail to a different viewpoint. These views don't quite compare with being right there, but it's still awe-inspiring.

The first part of the longer viewpoint trail is well-defined, but the last part goes over slickrock marked by cairns. There is no sign marking the end of the trail, but you'll know when to stop. At the end of the trail, you're at the edge of a steep cliff dropping down into Winter Camp Wash. You can't hike to the arch from this point.

7 FIERY FURNACE

Type of trail:	Loop.
Type of trip:	Ranger-led day hike.
Total distance:	2 miles.
Elevation change:	150 feet.
Time required:	2-3 hours.
Maps:	Trails Illustrated Arches National Park and USGS Arches National Park.
Difficult:	Moderate (ranger-led trips) or difficult (self exploration).
Starting point:	Fiery Furnace Parking Area.

Finding the trailhead: To find the trailhead, drive north into the park on the main road for 14.5 miles and turn right (east) at the well-signed Fiery Furnace road (just after the Salt Valley Overlook). Park in the Fiery Furnace Parking Area, which is a short drive from the main road.

The hike: To see the Fiery Furnace area of Arches National Park, you can take a ranger-led tour or take an off-trail adventure on your own. In either case, stop at the visitor center when entering the park to get a permit or to make a reservation for the guided tour. In any case, be sure to take water.

Incidentally, the area was not named for its average temperature. Actually, it belies its name and remains fairly cool even in midsummer due to the many shady canyons. Instead, the area was named for the reddish glow it often takes on at sunset which resembles a furnace.

After a brief orientation talk, a ranger leads the guided tour down one of the trails leaving the parking area. Three hours later, you return to the parking area on the other trail. As you walk along the 2-mile loop, the ranger explains the incredible natural history of the area and points out rare plants and semi-concealed arches.

The Fiery Furnace has suffered from its popularity. As a result, the NPS imposed special restrictions in 1994 in an attempt to curb a disturbing amount of damage to the fragile resources of the area. If you elect to go exploring on

Interpretive rangers lead daily tours into Fiery Furnace.

your own you must talk to a ranger who will help you understand the problems of overuse and discuss getting a permit. The area is a labyrinth of narrow sandstone canyons, and there are no marked trails, making it very difficult to stay oriented.

Two defined trails leave the trailhead, but they soon melt away into a fascinating puzzle of crevasses, fins, and boulders. This maze of canyons may be one of the most difficult areas to hike in the park, but it's also one of the most remarkable. The scenery, especially the steep-sided canyons and weird-shaped rocks, along with several arches and bridges, is unforgettable. You can also find a totally quiet place in the Fiery Furnace to help you forget the stress in your life.

The Fiery Furnace also provides critical habitat for many rare plant species, such as the Canyonlands biscuitroot, so please be intensely careful not to step on black-crusted cryptobiotic soil (desert topsoil) or delicate plant communities. Try to walk exclusively on rock or in sandy washes.

In 1997, the NPS will start charging a fee for both ranger-led tours and permits in the Fiery Furnace area.

8 SAND DUNE ARCH

Type of trail:	Out-and-back.
Type of trip:	Short day hike.
Total distance:	0.5 mile.
Elevation change:	Minimal.
Time required:	15-30 minutes.
Maps:	Trails Illustrated Arches National Park and USGS Arches National Park.
Difficulty:	Easy.
Starting point:	Broken Arch/Sand Dune Arch Parking Area.

Finding the trailhead: To find the trailhead, drive north into the park

SAND DUNE ARCH, BROKEN ARCH, SKYLINE ARCH, DEVILS GARDEN

© National Geographic/Trails Illustrated

on the main road for 17.5 miles and park along the main road in the Broken Arch/Sand Dune Arch Parking Area.

The hike: Sand Dune Arch is an easy, short walk nicely suited for groups with children. Even on a hot day, kids will love this place.

Shortly after leaving the trailhead, you hit a junction with the lefthand trail going to Broken Arch. Go right to Sand Dune Arch. Until the junction, the trail is well-defined. After the junction, you enter a narrow canyon (actually the gap between two sandstone fins) and stay there until you see Sand Dune Arch off to your right.

The reason for this arch's name becomes obvious along the way. You walk through deep sand which can make footing difficult and progress slow. The trail ends right at the arch. Below the arch the sand has collected in a huge "sand box" that kids love. The area usually stays shaded and coolish, even on a hot summer day. It might be tempting to climb to the top of the arch, but please resist the temptation. Rangers frequently have to rescue people injured falling or jumping from the arch.

You can take a short walk over to Broken Arch from this trailhead, but it's better to see Broken Arch from the loop trail starting in Devils Garden Campground. Refer to Hike 9.

9 BROKEN ARCH

See Map on Page 47

Type of trail:	Loop.
Type of trip:	Short day hike.
Total distance:	1 mile.
Elevation change:	Minimal.
Time required:	30-60 minutes.
Maps:	Trails Illustrated Arches National Park and USGS Arches National Park.
Difficulty:	Easy.
Starting point:	Devils Garden Campground across from campsite No. 40.

Finding the trailhead: To find the trailhead, drive north into the park on the main road for 19 miles and turn into the Devils Garden Campground. Go to the end of the campground and park along the small loop near the trailhead.

The hike: The trail, which starts at campsite No. 40 at the end of Devils Garden Campground, goes through sand dunes and slickrock to Broken Arch. In places the trail isn't well-defined, but well-placed cairns make it easy to follow all the way. The trail goes right through Broken Arch, a great place to take a break and study a great piece of nature's art.

You can retrace your steps back to the trailhead from here, but most hikers elect to take the loop trail that continues through the arch and comes back to the campground at campsite No. 51. Along the way, you'll see a trail coming in from Sand Dune Arch. If you're interested in adding a mile to your hike, you can take this trail out-and-back to Sand Dune Arch before completing the loop. At the end of this sidetrip, you have to walk about 0.25 mile on the paved campground road back to your vehicle.

10   SKYLINE ARCH

Type of trail:	Out-and-back.
Type of trip:	Short day hike.
Total distance:	0.4 mile.
Elevation change:	Minimal.
Time required:	15-30 minutes.
Maps:	Trails Illustrated Arches National Park and USGS Arches National Park.
Difficulty:	Easy.
Starting point:	Skyline Arch Parking Area.

See Map on Page 47

Finding the trailhead: To find the trailhead, drive north into the park on the main road for 18.5 miles and park in the Skyline Arch Parking Area. If you see the Devils Garden Campground or Trailhead, you've driven just past the Skyline Arch Parking Area.

Skyline Arch.

The hike: This is a very easy walk. It's only 0.2 mile to Skyline Arch on a flat, well-defined trail.

True to its name, Skyline Arch dominates the horizon for most of the trip. When you get there, you can see where a mammoth boulder fell out of the arch on a cold November night in 1940, greatly enlarging the size of the opening. This essentially doubled the size of the arch.

At the base of the arch, it looks as though a trail goes off to your left (north), but this isn't an official trail and doesn't go anywhere. This is a good example of why the NPS encourages hikers to stay on official trails. In the area around Skyline Arch, hikers who should have stayed on the official trail have created several well-defined "social trails."

11 DEVILS GARDEN

See Map on Page 47

Type of trail:	Out-and-back or loop.
Type of trip:	Short (to Landscape Arch) or moderately long day hike (primitive loop).
Total distance:	2 miles to Landscape Arch, 4 miles to Double O Arch, or 7.2 miles to Double O Arch returning by the Primitive Loop Trail, including all spur trails to points of interest.
Elevation change:	Minimal.
Time required:	1-4 hours depending on length of hike.
Maps:	Trails Illustrated Arches National Park and USGS Arches National Park.
Difficulty:	Easy (to Landscape Arch), moderate (to Double O Arch and on the Primitive Loop Trail).
Starting point:	Devils Garden Trailhead Parking Area.

Key points:

- 0.25 Spur trail to Tunnel and Pine Tree arches.
- 0.8 Landscape Arch.
- 1.0 Wall Arch.
- 1.4 Navajo Arch.
- 1.5 Partition Arch.
- 2.0 Double O Arch.
- 2.1 Junction with Primitive Loop Trail.
- 2.5 Dark Angel.
- 2.9 Private Arch.
- 6.2 Junction with main trail.
- 7.2 Devils Garden Trailhead.

Finding the trailhead: To find the trailhead, drive north into the park on the main road for 19 miles and park in the large parking area at the Devils Garden Trailhead. The trailhead is at the end of the road where it

The truly amazing Landscape Arch on the Devils Garden Trail.

makes a small loop. Be sure to stay on the loop instead of turning into the Devils Garden Campground.

The hike: If you take the Primitive Loop Trail and all of the short spur trails to nearby arches and other features, this becomes the longest hike on maintained trails in Arches National Park. It's also one of the most spectacular hikes you can take in any national park.

You can hike the entire loop in about 3 hours, but you could—and probably should—spend an entire day checking out the area and relaxing along the way. In any case, be sure to carry extra water. Also, you might want to get up early to take this hike to beat the heat—and to be sure you find a parking spot in the large but heavily used parking area.

About 0.25 mile from the trailhead, the trail splits. To go to Landscape Arch and Double O Arch and to complete the loop, take the left-hand fork. The right-hand fork takes you on a short spur trail down to Pine Tree and Tunnel arches. If you take this spur trail, it splits again at the bottom of a small hill. Go left to Pine Tree Arch and right to Tunnel Arch. After checking out these two large arches, head back to the main trail.

About a mile down the main trail, just before you see Landscape Arch and as you descend a series of steps, you see where the Primitive Loop Trail comes in. You can take the loop either way, of course, but this description covers the clockwise route, so take a left at this junction and continue to Landscape Arch.

The hike to Landscape Arch (2 miles out-and-back) is akin to the trip to Delicate Arch. It's one of those must-see features of Arches National Park.

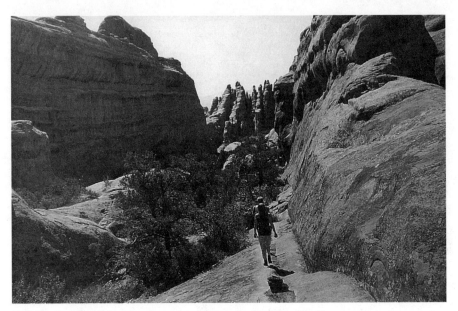

Hiking the Primitive Loop section of Devils Garden Trail.

This first part of the Devils Garden hike is a "super-trail"—flat, easy, double-wide, and usually heavily populated with hikers. Landscape Arch has an opening spanning an incredible 306 feet, which may be the longest stone span in the world. On the geologic time scale, Landscape Arch is a senior citizen among arches in the park. The arch is also famous for the extreme slenderness of its stone span. Don't wait too long to see Landscape Arch. Geologically speaking, it's likely to collapse any day.

Many people interested in a short hike turn back at Landscape Arch. If you have the time and energy, however, the trail ahead has much more to offer.

After Landscape Arch the trail gets less defined and stays that way. In fact, right after Landscape Arch the trail gets primitive for a short stretch, where it climbs over sandstone slabs and is marked with cairns. It's still easy to follow, though, and the trail all the way to Double O Arch gets lots of use. In this section, you pass Wall Arch on your right. As at Landscape Arch, you don't have to leave the main trail to see Wall Arch.

Another 0.25 mile up the trail, you'll see a short spur trail going off to the left to Partition and Navajo arches. Partition Arch is the arch you can see in the background when you're looking at Landscape Arch. Yes, Partition Arch has a partition, and the spur trail goes right up under the arch and ends, a great place to relax and soak in the view.

The trail to Navajo Arch also stops right under the arch, another great place for a break. This arch is shaded and perhaps an even better place than Partition Arch to stop and relax before continuing to Double O Arch.

When you get back on the main trail, it's another 0.5 mile to Double O Arch on a fairly rough trail, mostly on slickrock and a little hard to follow.

Double O Arch is most unusual, one arch on top of another. Just after Double O Arch you hit a junction with a spur trail heading to the left to the Dark Angel. Taking this spur trail adds nearly a mile to your trip, but it's worth it to get a close look at this blackish sandstone spike jutting out of the desert landscape.

Also right after Double O Arch, the Primitive Loop Trail heads off to the right. The NPS has marked it "Caution, Primitive Trail, Difficult Hiking," and the loop section of this hike is about as difficult as the section between Landscape and Partition arches which you have already hiked. In winter, some sections can be wet or icy making footing quite slick. If you turn back at this point, you will have seen most of the famous features of the Devils Garden Trail.

About a half-mile up the primitive loop trail, watch for a short spur trail going off to the right to Private Arch, the last arch you'll see on this loop. From here, instead of going from arch to arch like the first part of this trip, the loop trail traverses a beautiful desert environment where you can study the flora and fauna—and probably have it all to yourself. Even though many thousands of hikers take the first part of this loop trip, most people choose to retrace their steps on a better trail than brave the primitive loop route.

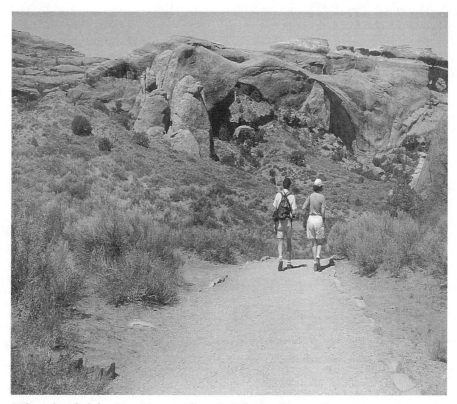

Hikers headed for Pine Tree Arch on Devils Garden Trail.

12   TOWER ARCH

Type of trail:	Out-and-back.
Type of trip:	Short day hike.
Total distance:	2.4 miles.
Elevation change:	Minimal.
Time required:	1.5-2.5 hours.
Maps:	Trails Illustrated Arches National Park and USGS Arches National Park.
Difficulty:	Moderate.
Starting point:	Tower Arch Trailhead.

Finding the trailhead: To find the trailhead, turn left (west) onto the Salt Valley Road which leaves the main road 16 miles beyond the entrance station. Follow the road for 7.1 miles until you see a junction with a sign pointing to a left turn to Klondike Bluffs. Take this road for 1.5 miles until it ends at the Tower Arch Trailhead. Be careful not to take the left turn (which leads to a difficult four-wheel-drive road) just before the Klondike Bluffs Road.

The hike: Tower Arch is a short, but rugged hike, or as indicated by the sign at the trailhead, a "primitive trail."

The trail immediately starts to climb to the top of the bluff, up a steep, but short, incline. After this brief climb, the trail continues up and down until you see massive Tower Arch surrounded by a maze of spectacular

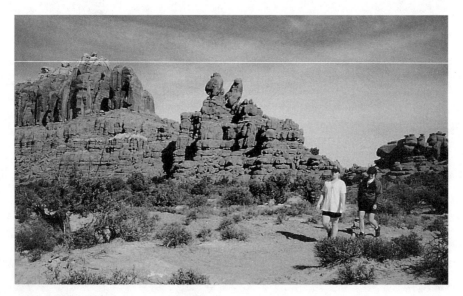

Hiking to the Tower Arch with Klondike Bluffs in background.

TOWER ARCH

© National Geographic/Trails Illustrated

sandstone spires. Along the way you get great views of the austere Klondike Bluffs on your right.

Part of the trail is on slickrock, so always be watching for the next cairn. The roughest part of the trail, however, goes through two stretches of loose sand near the end of the hike that make hiking uphill difficult. It's easy coming back, though.

You can climb up under the arch and get a great view while taking a deserved rest stop. In the spring, you'll see the magnificent, snowcapped La Sal Mountains to the east through the arch opening.

The return trip is noticeably easier than the way in. When you're at Tower Arch, you might see a vehicle just to the east. That's because you can drive around on a rough four-wheel-drive road, but those that do miss out on a great hike.

BACKCOUNTRY ROADS

1 WILLOW FLATS

Starting point:	Willow Flats turnoff on the main park road.
Finding the trailhead:	Drive 9 miles into Arches National Park and turn left (west) on the Willow Flats Road across from the Balanced Rock turnout.
Total distance:	4 miles from paved road to park boundary.
Time required:	1-2 hours.
Maps:	Trails Illustrated Arches National Park and USGS Arches National Park.
Permits:	No permit required.
Minimal vehicle requirements:	Low-clearance four-wheel-drive.
Difficulty:	Easy.
Road conditions:	Smooth driving on unpaved surfaces, mostly packed dirt, most of the way with a few short rocky sections and possible washouts after rains.
Suitability for mountain biking:	Moderate. The road can get seriously wash-boarded.
Vehicle campsites:	None.

2 SALT VALLEY

Starting point:	The Salt Valley turnoff on the main park road.
Finding the trailhead:	Drive 16 miles into the park and turn left (west) on the well-marked Salt Valley Road.
Total distance:	9.6 miles from the paved road to park boundary.
Time required:	2-3 hours.
Maps:	Trails Illustrated Arches National Park and USGS Arches National Park.
Permits:	No permit required.
Minimal vehicle requirements:	Low-clearance two-wheel-drive.
Difficulty:	Easy unless road surface is wet which makes the road impassable.
Road conditions:	Smooth driving on unpaved, packed dirt surface.
Suitability for mountain biking:	Excellent. The road can get seriously wash-boarded.
Hiking:	Access road for Hike 12: Tower Arch.
Special precautions:	Avoid this road after it rains. Sections of clay become seriously slippery when wet.

3 FOUR-WHEEL-DRIVE ROAD

Starting point: Salt Valley turnoff on the main park road.

Finding the trailhead: Drive 16 miles into the park and turn left (west) on the well-marked Salt Valley Road.

Total distance: 16.6 miles for entire loop, not including a 3-mile round trip to Tower Arch.

Key points:
7.1 Left turn on sign marked "four-wheel-drive road."
9.9 Spur road to Tower Arch.
12.0 Difficult stretch of loose sand.
14.0 Eye of the Whale Arch.
16.1 Willow Flats Road.
16.6 Main park road.

Time required: 3-5 hours.

Maps: Trails Illustrated Arches National Park and USGS Arches National Park.

Permits: No permit required.

Minimal vehicle requirements: High-clearance four-wheel-drive.

Difficulty: Easy to moderate with one difficult stretch between the Salt Valley Road and the Tower Arch turnoff.

Road conditions: The road conditions on the Salt Valley and Willow Flats roads are easy, but the connecting road has some difficult stretches. Shortly after turning off the

Driving the Four-Wheel-Drive Road between Salt Valley and Willow Flats with the Marching Men formation in the background.

Salt Valley Road, the road goes over a ridge with several tight turns, small ledges and long rocky sections. Drive this section slowly and carefully.

Suitability for mountain biking: Excellent on Salt Valley Road, but only fair on the four-wheel-drive road and difficult during one long section of loose sand at the 12-mile mark.

Hiking: If you take the short side road to Tower Arch, you should take the short walk into the arch.

Special attractions: Tower Arch and the view of the Marching Men from the junction of the four-wheel-drive road and the spur road to Tower Arch.

Special precautions: It's better to drive this loop in a counterclockwise direction so you can go downhill on one long section of loose sand. In fact, in summer months, you can't drive this road in a clockwise direction.

CANYONLANDS NATIONAL PARK: ISLAND IN THE SKY

OVERVIEW

Island in the Sky is a high mesa wedged between the Colorado and Green rivers like a natural observation platform. Vistas rival those found anywhere.

This district of Canyonlands National Park is the darling of the mountain biker, and mountain biking tours on the White Rim Road have become intensely popular; and during the peak seasons, campsites along the road are always full, having been reserved many months in advance. However, those without a mountain bike need not worry. The Island in the Sky also has lots to offer hikers, four-wheelers or casual tourists driving a rental car.

Although the trail system is not as extensive as in the Needles District, hikers can choose from a great variety of well-maintained trails. Trails dropping off the mesa and going to the White Rim Road are for the serious hiker, but the area also has easy and moderate hiking opportunities.

Many four-wheelers enjoy the White Rim Road and side roads, but these roads might not present a serious challenge for experts.

Tourists with only a day or two to spend here can get some fantastic scenery from the main paved roads in the park, and the brief visit can be supplemented with several excellent short hikes on the mesa (Grand View, White Rim Overlook, Mesa Arch, Aztec Butte, Whale Rock, or Upheaval Dome Overlook).

Rangers at the Island in the Sky Visitor Center (on your right about a mile past the entrance station) can answer your questions about the natural features and recreational opportunities found in the Island in the Sky District of Canyonlands National Park.

GETTING THERE

To reach Island in the Sky from Moab, drive north on U.S. Highway 191 10 miles to Utah Highway 313. To reach the same point, drive 22 miles south from Interstate 70. Once on Utah Highway 313, drive southwest 25 miles to the Island in the Sky entrance station.

ISLAND IN THE SKY

Type of trail:	Loop.
Type of trip:	Day hike.
Total distance:	5 miles.
Elevation change:	300 feet.
Time required:	2-4 hours.
Maps:	Trails Illustrated Island in the Sky and USGS Musselman Arch.
Difficulty:	Moderate.
Starting point:	Neck Spring Trailhead at Shafer Canyon Overlook.

Finding the trailhead: To find the trailhead, go 0.8 mile south of the Island in the Sky Visitor Center and turn left (east) into the Shafer Canyon Overlook parking area.

The hike: The Neck has historical significance. Here, the Island in the Sky plateau narrows to about 40 feet with sheer cliffs dropping off on both sides. This natural phenomenon allowed early ranchers who ran livestock in the area (before the park was created) to control the entire 43-square-mile mesa with one 40-foot fence across this narrow spot, later named The Neck.

Nature is also making a play at The Neck. Erosion is gradually wearing

NECK SPRING, GOOSENECK

© National Geographic/Trails Illustrated

Neck Spring Trail.

away the already-narrow entrance to the Island in the Sky. Sometime in the future, the Island in the Sky might really be an island.

One pleasant characteristic of the Neck Spring Trail is that it's a loop, one of the few in the Island in the Sky area. Most trails here are out-and-back or shuttles from road to road. This trail description follows the counterclockwise route. For more information, you can get a small brochure on the Neck Spring area at the visitor center or trailhead.

For hikers looking for a moderate, half-day hike this trail is ideal. The trail is well-defined the entire way, with good footing (only one small slickrock section) and only minor elevation gain. Parts of the trail parallel the main road, but you're far enough away that you hardly notice. You will notice, however, the panoramic views from the trail.

The Neck Spring area allows hikers to experience a wide variety of high desert habitats in a small area. In springtime, the area often turns into a wildflower garden, so wildflower buffs will love this trail.

After leaving the trailhead, immediately cross the main road and continue on the trail on the other side. The first part of the trail is actually an old road built by ranchers who used Neck Spring as a water source. Along this section of trail, you'll notice signs of past ranching activities, such as pipes and water troughs.

The trail then drops down in elevation and angles to the left to Neck Spring, but not directly to the spring. However, you can easily see it. It's tempting to bushwhack over to the spring, but please enjoy it from a distance. This trail gets heavy use, and this is a very fragile area.

From the trail you'll notice a change in the vegetation with species like

Gambel oak and maidenhair fern able to exist in this area with its extra moisture and shade. Also watch for hummingbirds, deer, and other wild animals who frequent the area.

After Neck Spring, the trail climbs slightly as you head toward the second major spring in the area, Cabin Spring. At the spring, you see the same type of vegetative change as you did at Neck Spring—and a few aging signs of past ranching activity.

Shortly after Cabin Spring, you face a short but steep climb up to the Island in the Sky mesa. The trail gets a little rough here, some of it on slickrock. When on top, you get a grand vista of Upper Taylor Canyon and the Henry Mountains off in the distance.

The last part of the trail follows the rim of the plateau directly above Cabin Spring and Neck Spring and through Gray's Pasture, a grassy bench used for cattle grazing until 1975. With no livestock grazing, the area's native grasses have begun to recover and now provide food for native species only.

After passing by the top of Neck Spring, you cross the main road again and follow the old road cut about 0.5 mile back to the parking area. Be careful crossing and walking along the road.

14 LATHROP

Type of trail:	Out-and-back.
Type of trip:	Day hike or overnighter.
Total distance:	To canyon rim, 5 miles; to White Rim Road, 10 miles; to the Colorado River, 18 miles (all round-trip distances).
Elevation change:	To the canyon rim, minimal; to White Rim Road, 1,600 feet; to the Colorado River, 2,000 feet.
Time required:	To the canyon rim, 2-3 hours; to White Rim Road, 6-7 hours; to Colorado River, 12-14 hours (round-trip times).
Maps:	Trails Illustrated Island in the Sky and USGS Musselman Arch and Monument Basin.
Difficulty:	To canyon rim, easy; to White Rim Road, difficult; to Colorado River, moderate.
Starting point:	Lathrop Trailhead.

CANYON RIM

HEAD OF LATHROP CANYON

WHITE RIM ROAD

COLORADO RIVER (4,000 ft.)

FT. 4000 4500 5000 5500 6000 6500

MILES 1 2 3 4 5 6 7 8 9

LATHROP

© National Geographic/Trails Illustrated

Finding the trailhead: To find the trailhead, go 2.2 miles south of the Island in the Sky Visitor Center and park on the turnoff on the left (east) side of the road at the Lathrop Canyon Trailhead sign.

The hike: The Lathrop Trail is significantly different than the other trails that leave the Island in the Sky for the White Rim Road. It goes 2.5 miles on top of the mesa before the trail heads down toward the White Rim, and the climb back up is more gradual than the Wilhite, Gooseberry, or Murphy Basin trails.

If you want a nice, flat, easy day hike, go to the canyon rim. After you take a break and enjoy the view, return to the trailhead. Another option is arranging a personal shuttle so you can be picked up on the White Rim Road, wisely avoiding the climb back up to the mesa.

The hike starts out through a flat grassland of peppergrass and ricegrass (both native species) with meadowlarks singing in the background and not even a juniper to break up the grassy sea. After a mile, you leave the ocean of grass and head off over mostly slickrock with a few stretches of loose sand and drop gradually in elevation until you reach the canyon rim. Here, you get a grand view of Lathrop Canyon and a glimpse of the mighty Colorado River far below. You can also see the White Rim Road and the well-named Airport Tower, a dominant landmark off to your right.

First part of the Lathrop Trail goes through a pleasant and unusually flat grassland.

The trail doesn't drop right off the rim into a series of switchbacks (as other trails from the mesa do). Instead, it angles off to the right (south) on a ledge and then starts switchbacking gradually down a side canyon to Lathrop Canyon. You can see the trail far below as you gradually drop down to it.

After about a mile on the old jeep road, the trail heads east on a little ridge between two canyons for about a half mile and then drops into the dry wash of one of them, which is where you stay for the last half-mile or so to the White Rim Road. When you get there, find a nice rock to sit on and marvel at the awesome Airport Tower and the beautiful cliffs you just came down—and, of course, start thinking about climbing back up (unless you bribed somebody to pick you up or leave your vehicle here).

Backpacking is not allowed above the White Rim Road in the Lathrop and Gooseberry areas, but you can camp below the road in Lathrop Canyon (as long as you ask a ranger about the specifics of this backpacking zone and get the permit at the visitor center in advance). Then, you can hike down to the Colorado River the next day. It's 4 miles from the road on a four-wheel-drive road. There's a great place to take a long break at the end of the road, a picnic area with three tables and a vault toilet all nestled under a grove of willows and cottonwoods. The road is easy walking after you drop below the cliffs (at the top of the road).

Even though you might be tempted, you can't camp at the end of the road near the picnic tables. This violates park regulations, and since it's in a big

Picnic area along the Colorado River at end of Lathrop Canyon Road.

wash, it can be dangerous, too. Don't be too daunted at the cliffs as you walk back. Remember how easy the descent was, which means the ascent is not too strenuous.

15   MESA ARCH

See Map on Page 67

Type of trail:	Loop.
Type of trip:	Day hike.
Total distance:	0.5 mile.
Elevation change:	Minimal.
Time required:	30-60 minutes.
Maps:	Trails Illustrated Island in the Sky and USGS Musselman Arch.
Difficulty:	Easy.
Starting point:	Mesa Arch Trailhead.

Finding the trailhead: To find the trailhead, go 6.3 miles south of the Island in the Sky Visitor Center and turn left (east) into the Mesa Arch parking area.

The hike: This is a perfect trail for beginners. It's easy and short, and a detailed display at the trailhead explains how to hike the trail.

Even though the NPS manages this trail for beginners, it has something

Hikers taking a break at Mesa Arch where they get a sweeping view of the White Rim east of Island in the Sky.

for everybody. Signs identify key plant species along the way, and half way along the short loop, you are treated to spectacular Mesa Arch. The arch is right on the edge of a 500-foot cliff, part of a 1,200-foot drop into Buck Canyon. You can get a keyhole view of the White Rim country through the arch, and if you step back a few steps, you can also frame the lofty La Sal Mountains (usually snow-topped in the spring) with the arch.

The trail is well marked and partly on slickrock. It's an easy hike, but if you have children along, carefully watch them when around the arch. There is no fence to prevent a sure-to-be-fatal fall. Do not climb on the arch.

If you look carefully, you can also see another arch from Mesa Arch Overlook—Washer Woman Arch—off to the left when facing the arch.

Type of trail:	Out-and-back.
Type of trip:	Day hike.
Total distance:	1.5 miles (round-trip).
Elevation change:	200 feet.
Time required:	1-1.5 hours.
Maps:	Trails Illustrated Island in the Sky and USGS Musselman Arch and Upheaval Dome.
Difficulty:	Moderate.
Starting point:	Aztec Butte Trailhead.

Finding the trailhead: To find the trailhead, drive 6.5 miles south of the Island in the Sky Visitor Center and turn right (west) at the Upheaval Dome Road and go another 0.8 mile and turn right (north) into the Aztec Butte parking area.

The hike: This hike can be deceptively difficult. The first two-thirds of the trail are well-defined and on packed sand, but near the end of the hike, you follow cairns as you climb about 200 feet up a difficult slickrock slope. Make sure you have appropriate shoes, and be careful.

The climb up the slickrock slope to the top of the butte is more difficult than ascending Whale Rock, and there are no handrails.

Once on top, you can see a structure called a granary. Don't touch or enter the structure. You can also enjoy some great vistas, particularly the view toward the headwall of massive Trail Canyon to the northwest.

MESA ARCH, AZTEC BUTTE, WILHITE

© National Geographic/Trails Illustrated

Aztec Butte.

On the way back, you can climb up and around the top of a similar butte between Aztec Butte and the trailhead. The hike is similar to the one to Aztec Butte, but shorter and easier. If you want to take this option, watch for a trail veering off to the west just before you start going around the other, unnamed butte.

17   WILHITE

See Map on Page 67

Type of trail:	Out-and-back.
Type of trip:	Long day hike or overnighter.
Total distance:	10 miles (round-trip).
Elevation change:	1,600 feet.
Time required:	7-8 hours (round-trip).
Maps:	Trails Illustrated Island in the Sky and USGS Upheaval Dome.
Difficulty:	Difficult.
Starting point:	Wilhite Trailhead.

Finding the trailhead: To find the trailhead, go 6.5 miles south of the Island in the Sky Visitor Center and turn right (west) on the Upheaval Dome Road. Go another 2.1 miles to the Wilhite parking area at the trailhead sign on the left (south) side of the road.

The hike: Like other trails leaving the Island in the Sky, the Wilhite hike includes a big hill. Even though the Gooseberry Trail has the reputation of being the toughest climb in the Island in the Sky District, the Wilhite has more elevation change (1,600 feet compared to 1,400 feet for Gooseberry). However, that elevation change is spread out over more miles of trail.

The first mile of the hike is easy walking on nicely defined trail with a few short sections of loose sand and slickrock. Then, the trail veers off to the right at the top of the headwall of Holeman Spring Canyon. Like other trails that drop over the "edge of the sky" the view can be somewhat daunting when you realize you have to climb down and then, later, up the steep cliff. However, looks can be deceiving. The NPS has expertly routed the trail down the canyon wall to make it safe and used stairs and switchbacks to minimize the steep grade. All the way down you get great views of expansive Holeman Spring Basin.

At the bottom of the big descent, the trail follows the flat, blackbrush-dotted flats for about a half-mile before angling off to the left toward awesome Candlestick Butte. The trail then follows the rim of a canyon for another half mile before dropping off the rim to the north toward Steer Mesa and then into the dry wash of a small, unnamed canyon.

The trail follows the canyon bottoms the rest of the way. In some sections, cairns are scarce, but don't fret, the trail stays in the dry wash the entire last 2 miles to the White Rim Road. If you're backpacking, you can

Mountain bikers and support vehicle parked at the junction with White Rim Road and Wilhite Trail for a short hike down a slot canyon that starts at this point.

easily find a campsite in this area, but be sure to camp out of the wash for your own safety.

When you hit the road, the dry wash you've been hiking turns into a beautiful slot canyon. If you have some energy left, hike down the slot canyon. It's cool down there, and you can usually find pools of water. If you're staying overnight in the area, this makes a great day hike.

On the way back, don't fall asleep on your feet and get in the wrong canyon wash. The canyon the trail follows forks several times. Go left at the first two forks, right on the next two, then one more left turn before climbing out of the dry wash. Each of the forks is clearly marked with cairns, but if you suddenly wake up and realize you haven't seen a cairn for a while, you could have taken the wrong turn. If so, backtrack to the last fork and watch for cairns. Also, be alert not to miss the last turn out of the canyon. The trail takes a sharp right, and it's easy to miss it and continue up the dry wash.

18   ALCOVE SPRING

Type of trail:	Out-and-back.
Type of trip:	Long day hike or overnighter.
Total distance:	10 miles (round-trip).
Elevation change:	1,300 feet.
Time required:	6-7 hours (round-trip).
Maps:	Trails Illustrated Island in the Sky and USGS Upheaval Dome.
Difficulty:	Difficult.
Starting point:	Alcove Spring Trailhead.

ALCOVE SPRING

Finding the trailhead: To find the trailhead, go 6.5 miles south of the Island in the Sky Visitor Center and turn right (west) on the Upheaval Dome Road. Go another 3.3 miles to the Alcove Spring parking area at the trailhead sign on the right (north) side of the road.

The hike: The Alcove Spring Trail starts dropping immediately, but not as steeply as the "big drops" of Wilhite, Murphy, and Gooseberry. The first mile of the trail coming down from the Island in the Sky is a little rocky, but there are lots of steps installed to make coming down and climbing back up easier. The last 4 miles is easy "wash walking."

The trail gradually switchbacks down with one long stretch along an absolutely massive cliff with an enormous, amphitheater-like alcove for which the trail is named. After about a mile, the well-defined trail levels out, an-

ALCOVE SPRING, ALCOVE SPRING/SYNCLINE LOOP, WHALE ROCK, SYNCLINE LOOP, UPHEAVAL DOME OVERLOOK, UPHEAVAL CANYON, MOSES

© National Geographic/Trails Illustrated

The alcove on Alcove Spring Trail.

The Alcove Spring Trail goes through Trail Canyon with Moses and Zeus in the background.

gling to the left before heading down into Trail Canyon. In another mile or so, the trail dips into the dry wash of Trail Canyon and stays there until you reach the end of the Taylor Canyon Road. Trail Canyon is a big, broad valley with sensational cliffs on both sides.

Once you're in the dry wash, follow it the rest of the way. Some long stretches don't have cairns, but don't fret. The trail stays right in the dry wash. During the last mile you get great views of Zeus and Moses and Aphrodite, awesome spires of rock on the north horizon—and the darlings of rock climbers everywhere.

If you're backpacking, you won't have any trouble finding a good spot in Trail Canyon. You can also go up into Upper Taylor Canyon to camp.

Just as Trail Canyon merges with Taylor Canyon, the trail leaves the dry wash. This turn is easy to miss, so have your topo map out and watch for cairns at about two o'clock. From here, it's only about a quarter mile on a defined trail to the Moses Trailhead. If you miss this turn, you'll come out at Taylor Camp, and you can walk back from there about a quarter mile to the trailhead.

On the way back, the point where you leave the dry wash is well-marked with cairns so you shouldn't miss it.

19 ALCOVE SPRING/SYNCLINE LOOP

See Map on Page 71

Type of trail:	Loop.
Type of trip:	Multi-day backpacking trip.
Total distance:	19.6 miles (can be shortened to 18.4 miles)
Elevation change:	1,750 feet.
Time required:	14-18 hours.
Maps:	Trails Illustrated Island in the Sky and USGS Upheaval Dome.
Difficulty:	Difficult.
Starting point:	Alcove Spring Trailhead.

Key points:

- 4.7 Trail Canyon and Taylor Canyon merge.
- 5.0 End of Taylor Canyon Road and Moses Trailhead.
- 5.2 Taylor Vehicle Campsite.
- 5.8 The Big Draw.
- 9.9 White Rim Road.
- 10.0 Labyrinth Vehicle Campsite.
- 10.6 Upheaval Canyon Trailhead.
- 13.6 Syncline Loop/Upheaval Dome Loop Trail.
- 13.9 Syncline Backcountry Campsite.
- 18.4 Upheaval Dome Trailhead.
- 19.6 Alcove Spring Trailhead (on paved road).

Finding the trailhead: To find the trailhead, go 6.5 miles south of the Island in the Sky Visitor Center and turn right (west) on the Upheaval Dome Road. Go another 3.3 miles to the Alcove Spring parking area at the trailhead sign on the right (north) side of the road. The Upheaval Dome Trailhead is another 1.2 miles down the road.

The hike: Regrettably, the Island in the Sky District doesn't have many long backpacking loops. Instead, most of the long hikes here are out-and-back. However, you can create one very nice loop trip by combining the Alcove Spring, Upheaval Canyon and part of the Syncline Loop trails with sections of the Taylor Canyon Road and a short section of the White Rim Road.

This loop requires a minimum of two nights out, but three nights out would leave more time to enjoy the area. The loop can, of course, be taken in either direction, but this trail description covers the counterclockwise route.

There are two ways to shorten the trip. If you're fortunate enough to have two vehicles in your party, leave one at the Upheaval Dome Trailhead so you don't have to hike the last 1.2 miles on paved road back to your vehicle at the Alcove Spring Trailhead. Also, you can take the right (south) turn when you get to the Syncline Loop, which also cuts 1.2 miles off your trip. This route description takes the left (north) route.

The entire route of this backpacking trip is described elsewhere in this book (See Hike 18: Alcove Spring, Hike 21: Syncline Loop, Hike 30: Upheaval Canyon, Road 6: White Rim Road, and Road 8: Taylor Canyon.) However, you still need to plan out your overnight stays and side trips.

Fortunately, you have some great choices for both campsites and side trips. You can camp in several side canyons, but not at the designated vehicle campsites (Taylor Canyon or Labyrinth) which are reserved for vehicle campers. You can also camp at the Syncline Backcountry Campsite, and other options for overnight stays include camping in Trail Canyon, Upper Taylor Canyon, The Big Draw, Upheaval Bottom, and Upheaval Canyon.

A must-see side trip is to Moses, a 1-mile loop around the famous spire. Perhaps the best second choice is the 3-mile walk (round trip) into the Upheaval Dome Crater which leaves from the junction of Syncline Loop Trail and Upheaval Canyon Trail. You can also take side trips up The Big Draw, into Upper Taylor Canyon, and along the Green River. Here are a few suggestions for your itinerary.

When you get to the junction of Upheaval Canyon Trail and Syncline Loop Trail, plan on some extra time to figure out all the signs and trails in

LENGTH OF TRIP	OVERNIGHT STAY	MILES PER DAY	SIDE TRIPS
Two-nights	1—The Big Draw 2—Upheaval Canyon or Syncline Backcountry Campsite	1—6-7 miles 2—6-7 miles 3—6-7 miles	Moses Upheaval Crater
Three nights	1—The Big Draw 2—Upheaval Canyon 3—Syncline Campsite	1—6-7 miles 2—4-5 miles 3—3-4 miles 4—5-6 miles	Moses Along Green River Upheaval Crater

the area. There are at least two well-defined, but unofficial, trails that can get you off track. The officially designated Syncline Backcountry Campsite (fairly new and not on some maps) is off to the left (north) about a quarter mile from the first junction and right along the official trail taking the counterclockwise route around Upheaval Dome.

---

20   WHALE ROCK

See Map on Page 71

Type of trail:	Out-and-back.
Type of trip:	Day hike.
Total distance:	1 mile (round-trip).
Elevation change:	300 feet.
Time required:	1-1.5 hours (round-trip).
Maps:	Trails Illustrated Island in the Sky and USGS Upheaval Dome.
Difficulty:	Moderate.
Starting point:	Whale Rock Trailhead.

Finding the trailhead: To find the trailhead, go 6.5 miles south of the Island in the Sky Visitor Center and turn right (west) on the Upheaval Dome Road. Go another 3.9 miles to the Whale Rock parking area at the trailhead sign on the right (north) side of the road.

Handrails to help hikers get to the top of Whale Rock.

The hike: If you want a great view of the entire Island in the Sky area, take the short climb to the top of Whale Rock. From there, you get a 360-degree panoramic look at the entire region. Plan on spending some extra time at the top to study all the interesting geologic formations.

The trail goes over slickrock most of the way, but it's carefully marked with cairns and handrails. And yes, if you use a little imagination, this rock outcrop sort of resembles a big old whale.

21 SYNCLINE LOOP

See Map on Page 71

Type of trail:	Loop.
Type of trip:	Long day hike or overnighter.
Total distance:	8 miles.
Elevation change:	1,300 feet.
Time required:	5-7 hours.
Maps:	Trails Illustrated Island in the Sky and USGS Upheaval Dome.
Difficulty:	Difficult.
Starting point:	Upheaval Dome Parking Area.

Key points:

0.1 Junction with overlook trail.
1.5 Start of steep descent.
3.2 Junction with Upheaval Canyon Trail.
3.5 Syncline Backcountry Campsite.
8.0 Upheaval Dome Trailhead.

Finding the trailhead: To find the trailhead, go 6.5 miles south of the Island in the Sky Visitor Center and turn right (west) on the Upheaval Dome Road. Go another 4.8 miles to the Upheaval Dome Picnic Area at the end of the road. The trailhead is at the west end of the picnic area.

The hike: This trail is the best choice for a long loop in this district. With two exceptions (Neck Spring and Murphy), all other long trails in the Island in the Sky are out-and-back hikes.

Try for an early start, especially if you plan to cover it all in one day. This can be a long, hot day hike in canyon country. And be sure to bring plenty of water. The NPS recommends 1 gallon per person per day.

The entire Syncline area has a fascinating—and controversial—geological history. Some geologists call Upheaval Dome "the most peculiar structural feature in southeastern Utah." The origin of the dome is the source of endless debate. For some mysterious reason, rocks formerly buried a mile underground are now on the surface in the crater. The two most common theories—the "salt dome" theory and the "meteorite impact" theory—are explained in a brochure available at the trailhead and visitor center. This trail circles the mysterious crater.

About 100 yards up the trail, the Upheaval Dome Overlook trail goes straight, and the loop trails go to the left and right. If you're going the clockwise route, as described here, take a left.

The first 1.5 miles of the trail are very pleasant—flat, well-defined, and easy walking. Then, you start a steep descent into Upheaval Canyon. For the next mile, the trail drops abruptly. Some sections are rocky and rough with short switchbacks, but it's still easy to follow. Most of the 1,300-foot elevation loss occurs in this mile. This is a fairly good reason to take the route clockwise. You'll notice that the climb up to the trailhead on the other side of the crater is not quite as steep.

Follow the canyon wash for about another mile to the junction with the Upheaval Canyon Trail. Here, the Upheaval Canyon Trail takes a sharp left and heads off to the west toward the Green River. You take a right and head northeast up the Syncline Valley.

Immediately after the junction, you go up a short but steep hill that gets you out of the Upheaval Canyon dry wash and onto a defined trail. Just before the hill, the trail appears to split. You'll be tempted to take the right-hand fork which is level and avoids the steep incline. Sorry, this isn't the

The view from Syncline Loop Trail west toward Buck Mesa and Upheaval Canyon.

Some sections of the Syncline Loop Trail follow the dry wash.

official trail, so take a left and climb the hill. The right fork goes off to the east about 1.5 miles into the depths of the crater. (A nice side trip, if you have enough energy and time left).

After you get to the top of the hill, the trail goes by the designated Syncline Backcountry Campsite and then stays nearly level for about a half-mile as it follows a grassy bench along the streambed.

In about another half-mile, the trail drops into the dry wash of Syncline Valley and starts up a narrow canyon with massive Upheaval Dome on the right and the cliffs leading up to Buck Mesa on the left. This is a beautiful canyon highlighted by a few large cottonwood trees. In the spring, you might see intermittent pools of water.

For the next mile or so, you climb steeply and gain most of the elevation you lost a few miles back. Near the top of the canyon is one very steep stretch.

After the short steep section, the trail keeps climbing but gradual. You go through an area of lush and diverse vegetation, including a stand of tall trees. At about the 6.5-mile mark, the trail forks. A short spur trail going off to the right to a spring coming out of an alcove—a great spot for a lunch break.

From here, the trail continues to gradually climb all the way to the trailhead, sometimes following the canyon wash. In the last 1.5 miles, you go over some slickrock sections, some of them moderately steep, so be careful.

22   UPHEAVAL DOME OVERLOOK

See Map on Page 71

Type of trail:	Out-and-back.
Type of trip:	Short day hike.
Total distance:	1 mile.
Elevation change:	100 feet.
Time required:	30-60 minutes.
Maps:	Trails Illustrated Island in the Sky and USGS Upheaval Dome.
Difficulty:	Moderate.
Starting point:	Upheaval Dome Parking Area.

Finding the trailhead: Refer to Hike 20: Syncline Loop Trail.

The hike: This is a great way to observe and study the geological wonders of the Upheaval Dome area without taking the arduous 8-mile loop. In fact, you get a better view of the mysterious crater from this short trail.

About 100 yards up the trail from the parking lot, the loop trails break off to the left and right. Continue straight. The trail climbs the entire half-mile distance to the first scenic viewpoint located on a slickrock outcrop. The NPS has provided an excellent interpretive display at the end of the trail explaining the geology of the area.

The trail continues on to a second slickrock viewpoint that gives you an even better look at the Upheaval Dome area. This increases the length of

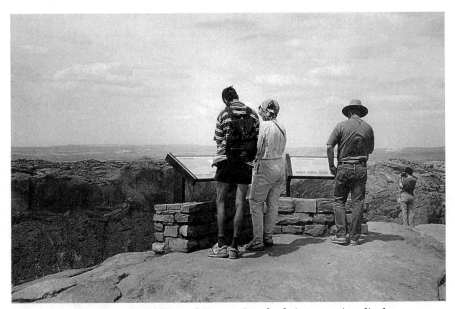

Hikers checking out the Upheaval Dome Overlook interpretive display.

the trip to 2.5 miles, but the trip between the first and second overlook is only a gradual upgrade.

Both unfenced viewpoints drop off sharply on the west side, so be careful and keep children under close supervision.

23   MURPHY BASIN

Type of trail:	Loop.
Type of trip:	Long day hike or overnighter.
Total distance:	10 miles.
Elevation change:	1,100 feet.
Time required:	5-7 hours.
Maps:	Trails Illustrated Island in the Sky and USGS Monument Basin and Turks Head.
Difficulty:	Difficult.
Starting point:	Murphy Trailhead.

Key points:

    0.5   Junction with Murphy Point Trail.
    1.5   Junction with Murphy Wash Trail.
    4.5   White Rim Road.
    4.8   Murphy Vehicle Campsite.
    5.8   Junction with Murphy Wash Trail.
    8.5   Junction with Murphy Hogback Trail.
    9.5   Junction with Murphy Point Trail.

Finding the trailhead: Drive 8.6 miles south from the Island in the Sky Visitor Center and park at the pullout at the Murphy Trailhead.

The hike: Unlike most trails in the Island in the Sky District, Murphy Basin is a nice loop instead of an out-and-back route. A pleasant mile-long walk on the White Rim Road connects the Murphy Hogback to the Murphy Wash trails to complete the loop. This trail description follows the counter-

MURPHY BASIN, MURPHY POINT

© National Geographic/Trails Illustrated

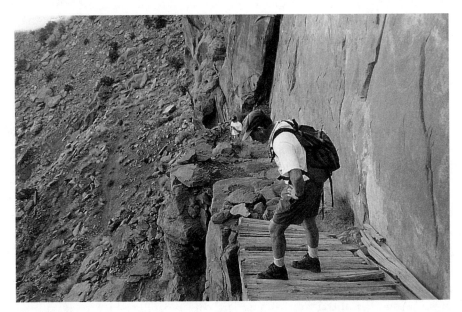

One place there was simply no place to put the trail down the Island in the Sky to Murphy Basin.

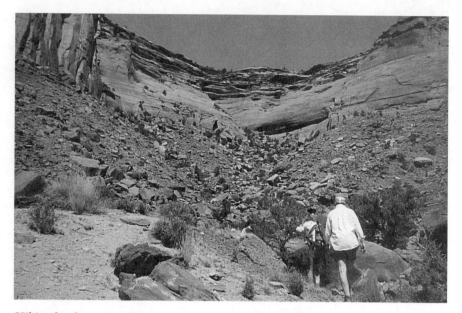

Hiking back to Murphy Point up the dry wash section of the trail with a big climb up to Island in the Sky just ahead.

clockwise route which allows you to walk down instead of up a hill on the White Rim Road.

From the trailhead, you follow a recently abandoned road for about a half-mile to the former trailhead and parking area and junction with the Murphy Point Trail. From here, the trail stays on the flat mesa for less than a quarter mile before heading down a 1,000-foot descent into Murphy Basin. Like other such descents from the Island in the Sky, the NPS has expertly routed and contoured the trail to make it safe and enjoyable walking. In one place, a wooden bridge was installed to securely cross a short steep spot.

Right at the bottom of the mile-long descent, the trail splits with the right fork following the hogback and the left fork dropping into the dry wash. Take your pick on which way you want to do the 8-mile loop section of this trail.

If you go right, you follow a flat, well-defined, packed dirt trail all the way to the White Rim Road. The trail stays on a small mesa and makes for pleasant walking.

When you reach White Rim Road, take a left (south). You'll see Murphy Vehicle Campsite and a vault toilet. Continue down the White Rim Road for about 2 miles until you see the sign for the Murphy Wash Trail which heads up the dry wash. The trail stays in the dry wash until just before the big climb back up to the Island in the Sky. The climb looks even more daunting from below than it did from above. The cliff looks like sheer rock with no possibility of a safe trail, but at the top, you'll probably say something to the effect that it wasn't half as hard as it looked.

24 MURPHY POINT

See Map on Page 81

Type of trail:	Out-and-back.
Type of trip:	Day hike.
Total distance:	4 miles (round trip).
Elevation change:	Minimal.
Time required:	2-3 hours.
Maps:	Trails Illustrated Island in the Sky and USGS Monument Basin and Turks Head.
Difficulty:	Easy.
Starting point:	Murphy Basin Trailhead.

Finding the trailhead: Same trailhead as Hike 23: Murphy Basin.

The hike: The Murphy Point Trail used to be the Murphy Point Road, which went to within 0.2 mile of the overlook. In 1996, the NPS converted the road to a trail starting at the Murphy Trailhead. (Some older maps may still show it as a road.) This created a nice 2-mile hike with an absolutely stunning view.

The trail is mostly flat as it stays on the same level as the Island in the Sky. Since you're walking on what used to be a two-wheel-drive road, it's easy going. About 0.2 mile from the point, the trail reaches the spot where vehicles used to park. The rest of the way is on an easy trail with some slickrock sections.

From the point, you get a breathtaking view of the White Rim Country west of Island in the Sky, including the Green River slowly making its way

The view from the end of the Murphy Point Trail.

to a grand meeting with the Colorado River a few miles later. Junction Butte dominates the southern horizon. You can see the White Rim Road curving along the White Rim Sandstone far below. Plan on spending some extra time here relaxing and soaking in the incredible expansiveness of the canyonlands.

You actually can spend the night on Murphy Point. The NPS has recently designated a backcountry campsite in the area. Ask about it at the visitor center. If a permit is available, you can park your vehicle at the Murphy Trailhead and hike about a mile into the Murphy Point area and spend the night.

25 GOOSEBERRY

Type of trail:	Out-and-back.
Type of trip:	Long day hike.
Total distance:	6 miles (round-trip).
Elevation change:	1,400 feet.
Time required:	4-6 hours.
Maps:	Trails Illustrated Island in the Sky and USGS Monument Basin.
Difficulty:	Difficult.
Starting point:	Island in the Sky Picnic Area.

Finding the trailhead: Drive 11.2 miles south from the Island in the Sky Visitor Center and turn left (east) into the picnic area. There is no trailhead sign on the main road.

The hike: When you look over the edge of Island in the Sky at the top of the Gooseberry Trail, it looks like you're getting ready to jump off a cliff. At this point, it's tempting to turn back, but you might be sorry if you do. This is a great hike.

This hike is perfect for the person who has been confined to a car for several days of sightseeing and now really needs some serious cardiovascular exercise. If you're a nontechnical climber, you can also hike this trail and then tell everybody you climbed to the Island in the Sky because that's exactly what you will do on this hike.

The trail drops 1,400 feet over the span of 3 miles. That might not seem too bad until you look at the topo map and see that you lose 1,300 feet of that elevation in less than 1.5 miles. It looks deadly, but the NPS has done a superb job constructing the trail to minimize the climb and make it as safe as possible. With a little caution, it's very safe.

GOOSEBERRY, WHITE RIM OVERLOOK, GRAND VIEW

© National Geographic/Trails Illustrated

The trail switchbacks down the steep side of the Island in the Sky formation and then drops into the dry wash for Gooseberry Canyon. While descending, watch your footing carefully—you can slip in some of the sections with loose sand.On the way down the hill, you get excellent views of the White Rim Country, and you can see the road ahead—perhaps with ant-sized vehicles driving on it. In spring, the white of the snowcapped La Sal Mountains merges nicely with the white of the White Rim Sandstone.

Once in the dry wash, it's easy hiking and nearly level until you reach the White Rim Road. When you get down to the road, you have to turn around and face the reality of getting back up to the picnic area. It can be a daunting sight but, again, it isn't that bad for anybody in reasonable physical condition. Take it slowly, make frequent rest stops to check out the scenery, and you might find it just as easy as coming down. The trail is the steepest in the last half-mile from the top, but still safe with all its little switchbacks.

When coming back up the arroyo for the first half of the trip, watch for the trail to take a sharp left and stairstep up the side of Gooseberry Canyon. If you aren't alert, you could continue up the dry wash and then have to backtrack.

The start of the Gooseberry Trail can be daunting.

Also, try to do this hike in the morning when the sun is not shining directly on the trail. If you start early, you can do the entire climb in the shade.

26 WHITE RIM OVERLOOK

See Map on Page 85

Type of trail:	Out-and-back.
Type of trip:	Day hike.
Total distance:	1.5 miles (round-trip).
Elevation change:	Minimal.
Time required:	1-2 hours.
Maps:	Trails Illustrated Island in the Sky and USGS Monument Basin.
Difficulty:	Easy.
Starting point:	Island in the Sky Picnic Area.

Finding the trailhead: Drive 11.2 miles south from the Island in the Sky Visitor Center and turn left (east) into the picnic area. There is no trailhead sign on the main road.

The hike: You can get a good view of the White Rim area from the parking lot, but a short enjoyable walk gives you a really good view. The White Rim Overlook trail starts at the right (south) side of the parking lot. It's flat and easy to follow the entire way. Some sections rely on well-placed

View of White Rim from White Rim Viewpoint.

cairns to show the way.

The trail ends at the end of a peninsula jutting out to the east from the Island in the Sky mesa. From the end of the trail, you can soak in an incredible panoramic view of the entire area. If it's near lunchtime, bring along a snack and a drink and have your lunch surrounded by the quiet beauty of the high desert before heading back to the parking lot.

27 GRAND VIEW

See Map on Page 85

Type of trail:	Out-and-back.
Type of trip:	Day hike.
Total distance:	2 miles (round-trip).
Elevation change:	Minimal.
Time required:	1-2 hours.
Maps:	Trails Illustrated Island in the Sky and USGS Monument Basin.
Difficulty:	Easy.
Starting point:	Grand View Point Overlook.

Finding the trailhead: Drive south from the Island in the Sky Visitor Center for 12 miles all the way to the end of the main road.

The hike: The NPS has placed several wonderful interpretive signs at the Grand View Trailhead, including a panoramic sign that names many of the prominent features in the area such as the Totem Pole, the confluence of the Colorado and Green rivers, and the White Rim Road winding its way around the Island in the Sky.

The trail is flat all the way, but it's poorly defined in spots. There are lots of cairns, but some are small. Be careful not to get too close to the cliffs. It's a long way down. If you have small children, watch them carefully.

At the end of the trail, you can sit and absorb a grand view, contemplating how nature transformed what was formerly a featureless plain into what you see today.

28 GOOSENECK

Type of trail:	Out-and-back.
Type of trip:	Day hike.
Total distance:	1 mile (round-trip).
Elevation change:	Minimal.
Time required:	20-30 minutes.
Maps:	Trails Illustrated Island in the Sky and USGS Musselman Arch.
Difficulty:	Easy.
Starting point:	Gooseneck turnoff on the White Rim Road.

See Map on Page 60

Finding the trailhead: From the entrance station, drive 6.4 miles on the White Rim Road and park at the parking area on the left (east) side of the road.

The hike: At this point on the White Rim Road, you'll have been bumping along on some of the rockiest sections of road, so a little hike might be just what you need. If so, the Gooseneck will be just right. This pleasant trail would be a great diversion from your mountain bike or four-wheeler.

This is a short walk, only about a half-mile one way. Take a snack and relax for a few moments at this very scenic overlook. You can see a huge sweeping meander in the Colorado River as it slowly heads south for its big meeting with the Green River just around the corner. You can also see a huge balanced rock right below the overlook, rivaling the famous balanced rock in Arches National Park.

The trail is mostly on slickrock, but numerous cairns clearly show the way. It's a slightly uphill grade to the overlook.

Type of trail:	Out-and-back.
Type of trip:	Day hike.
Total distance:	2 miles (round-trip) to the ruin; 3 miles (round-trip) to the cabin.
Elevation change:	500 feet.
Time required:	1-2 hours.
Maps:	Trails Illustrated Island in the Sky and USGS Horsethief Canyon.
Difficulty:	Moderate.
Starting point:	Fort Bottom Trailhead.

Finding the trailhead: From the entrance station, drive the White Rim Road in your high-clearance four-wheel-drive vehicle for 66.1 miles and park at the parking area on the left (west) side of the road. You can also reach the trailhead from the north, 6.1 miles from the park boundary, if you have a four-wheel-drive vehicle.

The hike: This is a very interesting hike with two different destinations. You can go down to the bottom where an old ranch building sits or you can climb up to the top of a small butte to check out an intriguing structure built by Ancestral Puebloans. Or, of course, you can do both.

The first part of the trail is a recently abandoned road, so it's very easy walking. About a mile from the trailhead, you go over a little divide made out of bentonite clay and then around the north side of the butte. Once on the other side, you can take a left and go up to the ruin (which you could see

Hikers climbing up to Fort Bottom Butte

FORT BOTTOM

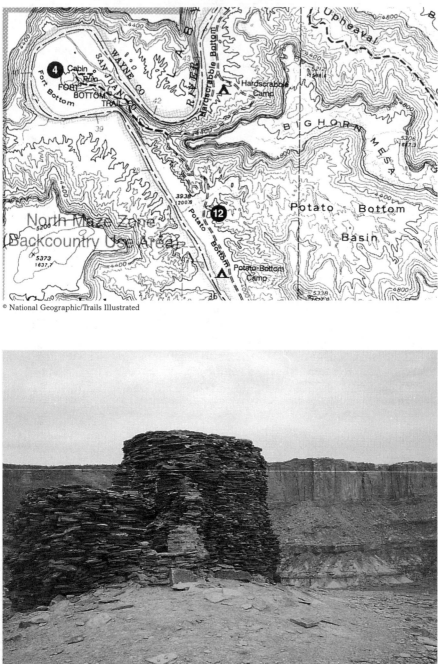

© National Geographic/Trails Illustrated

Tower structure on top of Fort Bottom Butte.

on the way down) or right and go down to the bottom, a site of the historic ranching operation.

If you opt to climb up to the top of the butte, the trail gets a little rough for about 100 yards, including two little cliffs you need to climb, but you can safely do so. Once on top, you can see the structure, but don't go in it or touch it. Tower structures are very common throughout the southwest. This is the only known tower structure within Canyonlands National Park.

The trail down to the bottom is easier, so if you have children, this might be a better choice instead of climbing up to the top of the butte. The trail to the bottom is easy all the way. When you get down there, you can see one old cabin and an area where a recent fire has destroyed some majestic old cottonwoods. You can also take a pleasant nap on the bank of the Green River.

30   UPHEAVAL CANYON

Type of trail:	Out-and-back.
Type of trip:	Day hike or overnighter.
Total distance:	6 miles (round-trip).
Elevation change:	400 feet.
Time required:	4-6 hours.
Maps:	Trails Illustrated Island in the Sky and USGS Upheaval Dome.
Difficulty:	Moderate.
Starting point:	Upheaval Canyon Trailhead on the White Rim Road (high-clearance, four-wheel-drive vehicle required).

See Map on Page 71

Finding the trailhead: From the entrance station, drive the White Rim Road for 69.1 miles and park at the parking area on the left (west) side of the road. You can also reach the trailhead from the north, 3.1 miles from the park boundary.

The hike: This is the longest hike on a trail accessed only by the White Rim Road. It's a great trail, mostly on packed sand. The first part of Upheaval Canyon is a broad open valley, and the trail cuts off the wide meanders. After the first mile or so, it drops into the dry wash. The broad valley you saw at the first part of the hike gradually becomes a narrow, twisting canyon just before you reach the junction with the Syncline Loop Trail.

31 MOSES

See Map on Page 71

Type of trail:	Out-and-back.
Type of trip:	Day hike.
Total distance:	2 miles (round-trip).
Elevation change:	500 feet.
Time required:	2-3 hours.
Maps:	Trails Illustrated Island in the Sky and USGS Upheaval Dome.
Difficulty:	Moderate.
Starting point:	End of the Taylor Canyon Road.

Finding the trailhead: To find the trailhead, drive to the end of the Taylor Canyon Road, park in the parking area, and walk less than a quarter mile east to the point where both the Moses Trail and the Alcove Spring Trail start and end. You need a four-wheel-drive vehicle to reach this trailhead.

The hike: This is a new trail not shown on many maps, but you can ask about it at the visitor center.

The trail climbs up and around the Zeus and Moses spires, and then goes through the little pass between Moses and a smaller spire called Aphrodite (unnamed on the maps), which gets you up close and personal to these awe-inspiring formations Have lunch on the little pass and enjoy views into both forks of Taylor Canyon.

It's a healthy climb to the base of the formations. Use caution hiking the loop around the formations. If you start thinking this is risky, think of the people who climb all the way to the top of the formations. They make this look like a walk in a shopping mall.

BACKCOUNTRY ROADS

4 GREEN RIVER OVERLOOK

Starting point:	Turnoff on Upheaval Dome Road.
Finding the Trailhead:	From the visitor center, it's 6.4 miles to the turnoff to Upheaval Dome. The Green River Overlook Road turns left (south) 0.4 mile later (same turnoff as Willow Flats Campground).
Total distance:	1.3 miles (one way).
Time required:	15 minutes.
Maps:	Trails Illustrated Island in the Sky and USGS Upheaval Dome.
Permits:	No permit required.
Minimum vehicle requirements:	Low-clearance two-wheel-drive.
Difficulty:	Easy.
Road conditions:	Excellent conditions on this well-maintained, unpaved road.
Suitability for mountain biking:	Excellent.
Hiking:	If you're camped at Willow Flat Campground, the short hike on the road to the overlook would be a great early morning or late evening stroll.
Vehicle campsites:	Road goes by entrance to Willow Flat Campground.
Special attractions:	Great vista of the White Rim country and, in the background, the Maze District. A skyline locator at the overlook helps you identify the major landmarks. The interpretive display at the overlook explains how John Wesley Powell explored Green River Country and found "cathedral-like buttes towering hundreds or thousands of feet and cliffs that cannot be scaled and canyon walls that shrink the river into insignificance." Today, you can float through this section of the Green River and still see the same thing—and be as impressed as Powell was.
Special precautions:	Although the overlook is partially fenced, watch children carefully.

5 SHAFER TRAIL

Starting point:	About a quarter-mile south of the Island in the Sky entrance station.
Finding the trailhead:	
Total distance:	6.6 miles (one way) to the park boundary.
Key points:	4.5 Bottom of switchbacks.
	5.1 Left turn to Moab and Potash, vault toilet.
	6.1 Shafer Camp.
	6.6 Park boundary.
Time required:	30-60 minutes.
Maps:	Trails Illustrated Island in the Sky and USGS Musselman Arch.
Permits:	Vehicle camping or backcountry permit required. Day use allowed without permit. People driving up the Shafer Trail from Moab must stop at the park entrance station and pay the park entrance/exit fee.
Minimum vehicle requirements:	High-clearance two-wheel-drive in dry conditions. Otherwise high-clearance four-wheel-drive. In winter carry chains.
Difficulty:	Moderate.
Road conditions:	Fairly easy driving with the exception of a few short rocky spots in the last 2 miles.
Suitability for mountain biking:	Excellent, but be careful going down switchbacks. Steep grade coming back up to entrance station.
Vehicle campsites:	Shafer Camp (one campsite).
Special precautions:	Be alert driving or mountain biking down the steep switchbacks in the first mile. Watch ahead and pull over if you see another vehicle coming up the switchbacks. Road conditions change if it rains or snows. When wet, you need a four-wheel-drive with chains.

6 THE WHITE RIM

Starting point:	About a quarter-mile south of the Island in the Sky entrance station.
Total distance:	72.2 miles within the park, plus another 24.6 miles to get back to your starting point.
Key points:	4.5 Bottom of switchbacks.
	5.1 Turnoff to Moab and Potash.
	6.4 Gooseneck Trailhead.
	8.2 Colorado River Overlook.
	8.4 Musselman Arch.
	16.2 Lathrop Trail.
	16.3 Turnoff to Lathrop Canyon.

17.3	Airport Tower Camp.
27.2	Gooseberry Trail.
27.7	Gooseberry Camp.
35.7	Turnoff to White Crack Camp (1.4 miles off the White Rim Road).
42.1	Murphy Wash Trail.
43.3	Murphy Camp.
43.4	Murphy Hogback Trail.
53.5	Candlestick Camp.
55.7	Wilhite Trail.
63.5	Potato Bottom Camp(A).
64.7	Potato Bottom Camp (B&C).
66.1	Fort Bottom Trail.
67.8	Turnoff to Hardscrabble Camp (A & B).
69.1	Upheaval Canyon Trail.
69.7	Turnoff to Taylor Canyon (5 miles to Taylor Canyon Camp).
69.8	Labyrinth Camp.
72.2	Park boundary.
76.0	Junction with Mineral Bottom Trail and spur road to Mineral Bottom Launch.
77.5	Top of switchbacks and parking area.
90.4	Utah Highway 313 and parking area.
96.8	Island in the Sky entrance station.

Time required: 15-20 hours.

Maps: Trails Illustrated Island in the Sky and USGS Musselman Arch, Monument Basin, Turks Head,

Mountain biking the White Rim Road near Airport Butte.

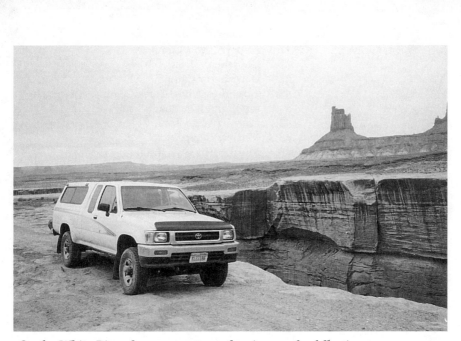

On the White Rim where you can see the view on the following page.

	Horsethief Canyon, and Upheaval Dome.
Permits:	Vehicle camping and backcountry permit required. Day use allowed without permit.
Minimum vehicle requirements:	High-clearance four-wheel-drive.
Difficulty:	Moderate.
Road conditions:	When dry, it's fairly easy four-wheeling most of the way, primarily on a packed dirt road surface with intermittent rocky sections. The section of road around Musselman Arch gets very rocky, and the sections over Murphy Hogback and between Potato Bottom and Hardscrabble camps are steep and hazardous when wet.
Suitability for mountain biking:	Excellent conditions most of the way with the exception of numerous but short rocky sections. Steep upgrades going up to Fort Bottom, Murphy Hogback, Shafer Trail, and near the end of the trip at Mineral Bottom. Remember that bicycles stay on the roads just like motorized vehicles.
Hiking:	While driving or mountain biking the White Rim, you'll probably welcome the diversion of getting out for a hike. Fortunately, you have many excellent choices, such as short walks to Musselman Arch and Colorado Overlook and an easy hike to Gooseneck Overlook (Hike 28) and moderate hikes to Fort

The view east from White Rim Road, looking toward the Colorado River.

	Bottom (Hike 29) and Upheaval Canyon (Hike 30). You also have several opportunities to hike back toward the Island in the Sky at Lathrop (Hike 14), Gooseberry (Hike 25), Murphy (Hike 23), and Wilhite (Hike 17). You might also try a nice off-trail excursion down a slot canyon that starts at the spot where the Wilhite Trail meets the White Rim Road. If you go up Taylor Canyon, try the short hike around Moses (Hike 31) or up Trail Canyon toward Alcove Spring (Hike 18).
Vehicle campsites:	All campsites along the White Rim Road have NPS-maintained vault toilets. Reservations are highly recommended as sites may be booked up to one year in advance:

Airport—Four campsites. Fairly exposed. Conveniently located for first night out on a multi-day mountain biking trip. In the shadow of Airport Tower. About 100 yards west of road.

Gooseberry—Two campsites. Exposed. About 100 yards west of road.

White Crack—One campsite. Exposed. Private (about 1.4 miles from the White Rim Road). Great view into Colorado River Basin.

Murphy—Three campsites. Right along road. Great view into Green River Basin.

Candlestick—One campsite. Exposed Great view of Candlestick Tower.

Potato Bottom—Three campsites. Right along road. Short level walk down to Green River.
Hardscrabble—Two campsites. Private. Short walk to the Green River.
Labyrinth—Two campsites. At junction with Taylor Canyon road. Exposed. Short walk to Green River.
Taylor—One campsite. Private. Great view of Moses and Zeus and Trail Canyon.

Special attractions: The White Rim Road is, for most people, a multi-day adventure. It has incredible scenery and world-famous mountain biking. The most popular way to see the White Rim Road is on a mountain bike, usually supported by a four-wheel-drive vehicle. Most people spend at least three days here to enjoy camping and hiking and to take spur roads into Lathrop and Taylor canyons.

Special precautions: Unlike many park roads, the White Rim Road gets extensive use during peak seasons. The NPS limits the amount of overnight use with the permit system, but currently day use is not limited. Watch carefully for other vehicles (especially on the steep sections on the Shafer Trail, on the Murphy Hogback, and Hardscrabble Hill near Fort Bottom) and for mountain bikers and hikers on the road. When wet, road conditions can dramatically worsen (especially around Fort Bottom). If you get caught in a rain, it might pay to wait 4-5 hours to let the road dry out. Also, be cautious around unfenced overlooks at the Gooseneck Overlook, Musselman Arch, and Colorado River Overlook. The NPS recommends that you carry chains and a shovel as well.

Be sure to take adequate water supplies. Store water in multiple containers—just in case one springs a leak.

7 LATHROP CANYON

Starting point: Junction of White Rim Road and Lathrop Canyon, 16.3 miles from the Island in the Sky entrance station.

Total distance: 4 miles (one way) from White Rim Road to Colorado River.

Time required: 30-60 minutes.

Maps: Trails Illustrated Island in the Sky and USGS Musselman Arch and Monument Basin.

Permits: At-large backpacking permit required. (This must be obtained at the visitor center.) Day use allowed without a permit.

Minimum vehicle requirements: High-clearance four-wheel-drive.

Difficulty: Difficult.

Road conditions:	Extremely steep at the head of the canyon near the White Rim Road. Few short slickrock sections. Sandy conditions near the bottom.
Suitability for mountain biking:	Mostly good with a few short stretches of loose sand.
Hiking:	You can hike off trail along the Colorado River.
Vehicle campsites:	None. Day use only. During high water, this area can be inaccessible.
Special attractions:	At the end of the road where it runs into the Colorado River, you'll find a great place for a picnic or lunch break, along with picnic tables, a vault toilet, and the shade of sprawling cottonwood, tamarisk and willow trees.
Special precautions:	Flash flooding potential extremely high when raining. Road conditions can change rapidly.

You might be tempted to jump in the river, but this is not a swimming pool. It's a big, powerful river.

8 TAYLOR CANYON

Starting point:	Junction between White Rim Road and Taylor Canyon Road, 2.5 miles from the north boundary of the park.
Total distance:	5 miles (one way).
Time required:	30-60 minutes
Maps:	Trails Illustrated Island in the Sky and USGS Upheaval Dome.
Permits:	Vehicle camping or backpacking permit required. Obtain at the visitor center. Day use allowed without a permit.
Minimum vehicle requirements:	High-clearance four-wheel-drive.
Difficulty:	Moderate.
Road conditions:	Excellent conditions with a few rocky sections. Road conditions can change rapidly when wet. Flash flooding potential. Deep sand exists when conditions are very dry.
Suitability for mountain biking:	Excellent conditions usually. Road conditions can change rapidly when wet. Flash flooding potential. Deep sand exists when conditions are very dry.
Hiking:	You should try the spectacular day hike around Moses (Hike 31) or hike up Trail Canyon toward Alcove Spring (Hike 18).
Vehicle campsites:	Taylor Camp (one campsite) at the end of the road in the shadow of the magnificent Moses formation.
Special attractions:	The famous Moses and Zeus spires make Taylor Canyon particularly popular with rock climbers.
Special precautions:	Don't try climbing the spires in the area without the proper training, equipment, and experience.

THE NEEDLES

CANYONLANDS
Island in the Sky

GLEN
CANYON
NRA

NATIONAL

The Maze

PARK

The Needles

Needles
Overlook

To
163

Elephant Hill

211

THE NEEDLES

To Newspape
Rock and

163

LEGEND

70 Interstate		Interstate Highway	
191 U.S. Highway		Paved Road	
211 State or Other Principal Road		Unpaved Road	
		4-wheel-drive Road	

THE NEEDLES

OVERVIEW

The Needles District of Canyonlands National Park is a high desert paradise, a jumbled landscape dominated by a series of distinctive sandstone spires called, of course, the Needles. Perhaps the other distinctive feature of the Needles District is an extensive trail system that offers nearly endless options for the hiker.

The Needles District has more hiking trails (about 55 miles) and a better variety of trails than the Island in the Sky or the Maze. In addition, this area is, in general, set up and managed for hikers with lots of loop trails and a good selection of easy or moderate hiking options as well as long, multi-night backpacking opportunities. Most trails have sections which go over slickrock, so get used to following cairns. In 1996, the NPS finished work on a designated backcountry campsite system.

The following pages include many suggested hikes, but the Needles District has so many trails and hiking options, that you can easily get out the map and find additional options. Rangers at the Needles Visitor Center are most helpful in suggesting a hike that might be just right for you.

For mountain bikers and four-wheelers, the Needles District might not offer as much as the Maze or Island in the Sky, but the area does have several backcountry roads. Some have well-placed scenic campsites, so visitors with four-wheel-drive vehicles can base camp and day hike from their backcountry vehicle camp.

The Needles District has a great visitor center about a quarter-mile past the entrance station. The Squaw Flat Campground has 26 campsites with picnic tables, pit toilets, fire rings (bring your own wood), and a water supply (spring through fall). The campsites go on a first-come, first-served basis, and you'll be lucky to get one during peak seasons. The Needles District also has 3 group sites which can be reserved in advance. Both individual sites in the campground and group sites have nominal fees.

The Needles District has more water than other sections of Canyonlands National Park or Arches National Park. In spring, you can often find a flowing stream in several canyons. (However, be sure to carry your own water instead of depending on unreliable desert water sources.) Also, in spring, the entire area can be awash with wildflowers.

GETTING THERE

From Moab, take U.S. Highway 191 south for 40 miles and turn west (right) on Utah Highway 211. Follow this paved road 35 miles to the Needles District Entrance Station. Be careful not to take the "Needles Overlook" road which takes off a few miles before the correct junction. This road does not take you to Canyonlands National Park. Watch for the Canyonlands National Park sign before turning. From Monticello, drive 14 miles north on U.S. 191, and turn west (left) on Utah 211.

HIKING AT NIGHT CAN BE A REAL DRAG

The Needles District attracts many thousands of hikers, some of whom are inexperienced. One fairly common (and serious) problem results is that less-experienced hikers underestimate how much time it takes to do a hike. Then, they get caught by nightfall and, in many cases, without a flashlight or head lamp.

Even with a flashlight or head lamp, following Needles trails at night can be very challenging. Most trails have slickrock sections and go along canyon washes, making it easy to miss a cairn and get off the trail. Be extra careful not to underestimate the time a hike will take or overestimate your physical abilities—especially when summer heat can significantly slow you down.

FRONTCOUNTRY TRAILHEADS

32   ROADSIDE RUIN

Type of trail:	Loop.
Type of trip:	Short day hike.
Total distance:	0.3 mile.
Time required:	20-30 minutes.
Maps:	Trails Illustrated Needles and USGS The Loop.
Difficulty:	Easy.
Starting point:	Roadside Ruin Parking Area.

Finding the Trailhead: Drive 0.6 mile from the Needles entrance station and park on the south side of the road in the well-signed Roadside Ruin Parking Area.

The hike: This hike offers an easy introduction to the Canyonlands and its cultural history and plant life. At the trailhead you can spend a quarter and get a brochure for this self-guided trail. The trail is well-defined and easy walking all the way.

Along the short, flat route, signs identify key native plant species, and a brochure (available at the trailhead) describes these plants and how Indians used them. At the end of the loop, you can see a granary typical of the structures found throughout the park, although few are as well-preserved as this one.

33 CAVE SPRING

Type of trail:	Loop.
Type of trip:	Short day hike.
Total distance:	0.6 mile.
Time required:	30-60 minutes.
Maps:	Trails Illustrated Needles and USGS The Loop.
Difficulty:	Moderate.
Starting point:	Cave Spring Parking Area.

Finding the Trailhead: Drive 0.9 mile west from the Needles entrance station and take a left (south) on a paved road (sign points to Salt Creek) and go 0.5 mile before taking another left (east) onto a dirt road. The unpaved road ends in 1.2 miles at the parking area and trailhead for the Cave Spring Trail.

The hike: If you're in the Needles area and have an extra hour, the Cave Spring hike would be an easy and pleasant way to spend it. The trailhead is conveniently located, and this short hike offers lots of diversity. You can

ROADSIDE RUIN, CAVE SPRING

© National Geographic/Trails Illustrated

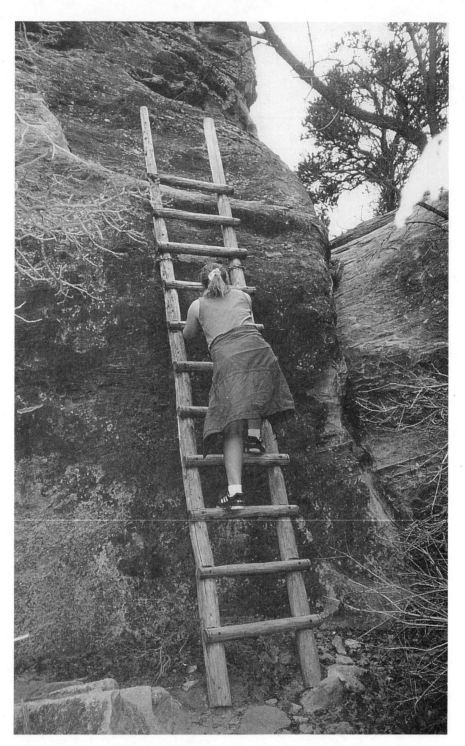

A ladder on the Cave Spring Trail.

pick up a brochure that explains the area's history and plant life at the trailhead.

The small loop trail goes by ruins of historic ranching operations active here until 1975 when grazing was abandoned in Canyonlands National Park. Please honor the barriers put up by the NPS to preserve this part of the area's history. Later, the trail goes by Cave Spring and then passes by some rock art left by the ancestral Puebloan Indians who inhabited the area 1,000 years ago. Please don't touch these rock art treasures.

After you finish enjoying the signs of both recent and ancient history, hike around a large "Canyonlands mushroom" and climb a safety ladder to a slickrock flat. Here, you get the experience of following cairns over slickrock and also get a great view of many of the area's main features such as the Needles, North Six-shooter Peak, and South Six-shooter Peak.

34   POTHOLE POINT

See Map on Page 107

Type of trail:	Loop.
Type of trip:	Easy day hike.
Total distance:	0.6 mile.
Time required:	20-30 minutes.
Maps:	Trails Illustrated Needles and USGS The Loop.
Difficulty:	Easy.
Starting point:	Pothole Point Parking Area.

Finding the trailhead: Drive 5.1 miles from the entrance station and park on the left (west) side of the road in the Pothole Point Parking Area.

The hike: If you need a little exercise or want to take small children for an easy, safe hike where they might learn something about desert ecology, Pothole Point would be an excellent choice. For a quarter you can buy a small brochure at the trailhead. The brochure explains the fascinating ecology of potholes.

Most of this hike follows a string of cairns over slickrock. The name Pothole Point comes from the numerous "potholes" that have formed in the slickrock along most of the trail. Once started, a pothole traps water after a desert rain. The rainwater is mildly acidic and ever-so-slowly enlarges the pothole. An intricate, symbiotic animal community featuring shrimp, worms, and snails, and perhaps even a Great Basin spadefoot toad gradually develops in some potholes. If you're lucky enough to visit Pothole Point shortly after a rain, you can observe these tiny ecosystems.

Over time, the wind continuously blows dirt, sand and small bits of organic material into the potholes. Eventually, plants take root in the thin layer of soil. The first sign of life in a pothole is often the cryptobiotic soil which provides the foundation for growth of larger plants. The end result is a "pothole garden," a pocket of miniature, bonsai-like vegetation in a bowl of solid rock.

You can hike this short loop in either direction. Watch for a spur trail going to the top of some big boulders where you can get a great view of the surrounding terrain in either direction, including the area's namesake, the Needles.

35   SLICKROCK FOOT TRAIL

Type of trail:	Loop (actually a "lollipop").
Type of trip:	Day hike.
Total distance:	2.4 miles.
Time required:	1-2 hours.
Maps:	Trails Illustrated Needles and USGS The Loop.
Difficulty:	Moderate.
Starting point:	Slickrock Foot Trail Parking Area.

Finding the trailhead: From the Needles entrance station, drive 6.4 miles and park on the right (north) side of the road at the Slickrock Foot Trail Parking Area, just before the end of the road.

The hike: If you're a beginning or experienced hiker with only a half-day to spend in the Needles District, the Slickrock Foot Trail would be a excellent way to enjoy it. Many hikes in the Needles follow canyon bottoms, but this trail stays high and gives an overall perspective of the entire southeastern corner of the Canyonlands National Park.

The NPS suggests this trail to inexperienced hikers so that they can get a look at the entire area before deciding where they want to go on their next trip. On this trail, beginners also learn how to follow cairns and hike on slickrock.

For the beginner who has only walked well-defined dirt trails, this hike might be a little adventuresome, but it certainly isn't dangerous. The trail is easy to follow with lots of cairns marking the way. Well-placed signs mark the way to four viewpoints and the point where the loop begins.

At the trailhead, spend a quarter to buy a handy brochure written for this hike. It describes much of the geology of the area and is keyed specifically to four viewpoints along the trail.

Take the hike counterclockwise as indicated by a NPS sign about a half-mile up the trail where the loop section of the trail begins. Viewpoint No. 1 is just before you get to the start of the loop. At this viewpoint, you get a nice panoramic view of the entire region and many of the major landmarks—Six-shooter Peak, Elaterite Butte, Cathedral Butte, the La Sal Mountains, Ekker Butte, and, of course, the Needles.

The trail stays on the ridge between Little Spring Canyon and Big Spring

POTHOLE POINT, SLICKROCK FOOT TRAIL, CONFLUENCE OVERLOOK

© National Geographic/Trails Illustrated

Canyon. At Viewpoint No. 2, you can get a good view into upper reaches of Little Spring Canyon.

After Viewpoint No. 3, the trail turns west and then south. You can take a long look at the region's namesake, the Needles, as you walk along.

Finding Viewpoint No. 4 is more difficult and time-consuming than the first three. It's about a quarter-mile walk to this viewpoint, whereas the first three were only 50-100 feet off the trail.

At Viewpoint No. 4, you can look down into massive Big Spring Canyon. In spring, you can see a stream flowing in the distance far below. The brochure gives you a great geology lesson from this viewpoint, so plan on spending extra time here to identify all the different strata making up the canyon's awesome cliffs.

After leaving Viewpoint No. 4, it's another mile or so back to the trailhead, most of the trail following the east flank of Big Spring Canyon.

36 *CONFLUENCE OVERLOOK*

See Map on Page 107

Type of trail:	Out-and-back.
Type of trip:	Long day hike.
Total distance:	11 miles.
Time required:	5-7 hours.
Maps:	Trails Illustrated Needles and USGS The Loop and Spanish Bottom.
Difficulty:	Difficult.
Starting point:	Parking area at end of main park road at the Big Spring Canyon Overlook.

Key Points:
1.2   Safety ladder.
1.5   Divide between Big Spring and Elephant canyons.
4.2   Four-wheel-drive road.
4.7   Four-wheel-drive road.
5.0   End of road.
5.5   Confluence Overlook.

Finding the trailhead: Drive 6.6 miles from the entrance station and park at the end of the road.

The hike: This is a serious hike, but the destination—a sweeping vista of the confluence of two great rivers—makes up for any discomfort in getting there. Some sections go over slickrock marked with strings of cairns, but unlike most trails in the Canyonlands, most of this trail is a well-defined dirt path. The NPS has expertly routed the trail through many interesting features, taking advantage of the great scenery along the way.

Immediately after leaving the trailhead, the trail drops steeply into Big Spring Canyon. Then, after about 25 feet in the dry wash, the trail climbs the other side of the canyon. Be careful not to take the well-used off-trail route up the canyon and miss the cairns going off to the right, marking the ascent out of the canyon.

The climb is well-marked with cairns, but footing can be a bit precarious in a few places. In one spot the NPS has installed a safety ladder. Once on top, take a break in a gorgeous spot where the trail goes through a small opening between two cliffs. Looking either way through this little "keyhole" gives you a great photo.

After leaving the keyhole, you stay high for about a mile. Here, you can see some well-sculpted and huge "Canyonlands mushrooms" before gradually dropping into expansive Elephant Canyon. Once down in Elephant Canyon, you follow a dry wash for about a mile, all easy walking. Then, you start a gradual climb out of Elephant Canyon—going by a giant red sand-

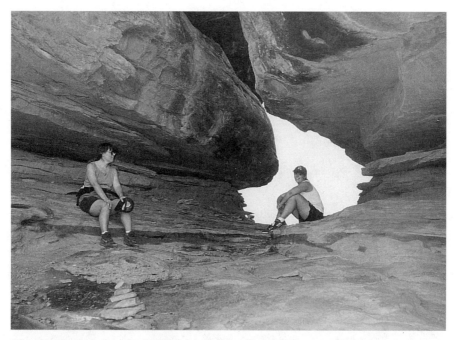

The Confluence Overlook Trail in the Needles District goes through a narrow "key hole" before dropping into Upper Elephant Canyon, a great place for resting and enjoying the high desert scenery.

stone spire with no name and into another big and equally beautiful drainage called Twin Valleys. From above you can look out and see the "twins," which almost look cultivated with a light-colored grass carpeting the valley floor.

Just as you get into Twin Valleys, you cross a four-wheel-drive road that goes north and south. The trail goes right across the road and continues on. The flat bottomland of Twin Valleys is carpeted with cheatgrass, a nasty, introduced species brought into the area when the area was heavily grazed (before the park was designated). Cheatgrass has completely taken over the area from native species, but its light green color contrasts nicely with the other green hues of the high desert.

After leaving the gentle grasslands of Twin Valleys, you crest a small knoll and drop into Cyclone Canyon, also invaded with cheatgrass. In Cyclone Canyon you cross the four-wheel-drive road again. This time, however, the trail turns into a road. (Some maps show this as a trail, but on the ground, it's a well-used road. Follow the road instead of looking around for the trail that isn't there.) Walk west 0.3 mile on the road, being careful not to take the north/south road through Cyclone Canyon. There are signs showing the way.

At the end of the road, you find a vault toilet and a picnic table and another sign informing you that it's still another 0.5 mile to the Confluence

Two mighty rivers, the Green and Colorado, merge below the overlook at the end of the Confluence Overlook Trail in the Needles District.

Overlook. It's a gradual climb to the overlook from here.

The overlook is incredible. You can see two mighty rivers merging. The Colorado's namesake carries on, and the Green River ceases to exist, at least in name. You also can get a good panoramic view to the west and north into the Maze and Island in the Sky regions of the park with Ekker Butte highlighting the horizon.

The overlook is unfenced, so don't to get too close to the edge. If you have children, watch them carefully.

On the way back, you'll notice that the NPS situated the parking lot in an appropriate location. You can see your vehicle from about a mile away as you come out of Elephant Canyon and head down into Big Spring Canyon.

SALT CREEK/HORSE CANYON TRAILHEADS

To get to the trailheads along these two backcountry roads, you need a high-clearance four-wheel-drive vehicle. Don't forget your permit. You need one for both overnight and day use in the Salt Creek and Horse Canyon areas.

The trailheads for Castle Arch and Fortress Arch are at the end of the Horse Canyon Road, and the route to Angel Arch begins at the end of the Salt Creek Road. The routes to these trailheads are described in detail on page 152. If you plan an out-and-back hike into Upper Salt Creek, start at a trailhead 1 mile from the end of the Salt Creek Road. If you plan to hike Upper Salt Creek one way as a shuttle hike, start at the Cathedral Butte Trailhead on Bureau of Land Management land just south of Canyonlands National Park, as described under Hike 37.

37 UPPER SALT CREEK

Type of trail:	Shuttle or out-and-back.
Type of trip:	Overnighter or long day hike.
Total distance:	14 miles (one way).
Time required:	8-10 hours (one way).
Maps:	Trails Illustrated Needles and USGS Druid Arch, South Six-shooter Peak, and Cathedral Butte.
Difficulty:	Difficult.
Starting point:	For the shuttle hike, park outside the park at the Bureau of Land Management's Cathedral Butte Trailhead. For the out-and-back hike, park at the trailhead 1 mile before the end of the Salt Creek Road.

Key Points:

1.8   Junction with Bright Angel Trail.
1.5   Canyonlands National Park Boundary.
3.5   Kirk Cabin.
3.7   Backcountry Campsites SC1 and SC2.
7.5   All-American Man.
8.3   Backcountry Campsite SC3.
8.5   Upper Jump.
12.0   Backcountry Campsite SC4.
13.3   Abandoned spur road.
13.5   Salt Creek Backcountry Road.

Diverse vegetation surrounds a spring along the Upper Salt Creek Trail.

Finding the trailhead: From the park entrance station, drive east out of the park on Utah 211 for 13.7 miles and turn right (south) on a gravel road marked "Elk Mountain and Beef Basin." If you're coming from the east, the turnoff is 20 miles from U.S. Highway 191. Follow this well-maintained, unpaved road for 17 miles until you see the small parking area on your right (north) with a BLM sign saying "Bright Angel and Salt Creek." This is officially called the Cathedral Butte Trailhead. There may be a gate across the road about 9.5 miles from Utah 211. You can open the gate and pass through, but be sure to close it behind you. You don't need a four-wheel-drive vehicle to get to the Cathedral Butte Trailhead unless it has recently rained, which can make the clay in the road very slippery. However, you do need a four-wheel-drive vehicle to get to the trailhead near the end of the Salt Creek Road. If you plan to stay overnight in Salt Creek or Horse Canyon, be sure to get your overnight permit at the Needles Visitor Center. You also need a day use permit for Salt Creek.

The hike: Names can be misleading. Somehow, "Salt Creek" seems to describe a dry, harsh, and unpleasant place when quite the opposite is true. Upper Salt Creek is definitely one of the most delightful hikes in the Canyonlands region, and it deserves a name like "Paradise Creek."

First of all, unlike most "creeks" in the region, this one is really a creek. A stream flows through much of the canyon. Because of the reliable source of water, early cultures inhabited the area, and rock art and ruins can be found throughout the canyon.

UPPER SALT CREEK

© National Geographic/Trails Illustrated

Secondly, this is not the typical, narrow canyon common in Canyonlands. Instead, it's a broad, flat, spacious valley with rich vegetative diversity ranging from cattail marshes to stately cottonwoods. And unlike many places in the park, Salt Creek has lots of wildlife—mule deer, coyote, bobcat and even the mighty mountain lion. You might not see them, but you can see their tracks in the sand and mud.

You can hike into Upper Salt Creek and back from the Salt Creek Road, but the best way to see this hidden corner of Canyonlands is to arrange a shuttle, starting the hike at the south end and having somebody meet you or leave a vehicle at the north end where the trail meets the Salt Creek Road. This means you can hike downhill all the way. If you did the shuttle route in reverse, it would be 13.5 miles uphill with a very steep grade at the south end as you climb up to Cathedral Butte Trailhead.

If you can't arrange this difficult shuttle, you can still enjoy Upper Salt Creek by making it a long day hike. If you go as far as Upper Jump (about 11 miles round trip from the Salt Creek Road), you'll only miss the broad expansiveness of the southernmost reaches of Salt Creek.

If you have three days, you can hike the 6 miles into Upper Jump, stay two nights at SC3, and then day hike upstream on your second day before going out on the third. You could go up to SC1 or SC2, but this would mean a four- or five-day trip.

But of all these options, the south to north shuttle is probably the best. Getting a ride to the Cathedral Butte Trailhead might be problematic, but it's worth it.

The Upper Salt Creek Trail in the Needles District winds through an unusually wide, flat high desert valley.

The Upper Salt Creek shuttle hike can be done in one long day, but to really enjoy "Paradise Creek," try for two or three days, as this trail description suggests.

The hike starts out in a juniper forest on a well-defined but rocky trail which drops sharply for the first 1.5 miles. At the 1.5-mile mark, you'll see a big open canyon on your left, the upper reaches of Salt Creek. The rather indistinct Bright Angel Trail from the west joins the main trail after you drop into the valley. You might miss this unmarked junction, but it doesn't matter.

After walking through the open canyon for less than a quarter-mile, you drop into the dry wash and see the park boundary signs. The NPS has put up signs on both sides of the dry wash so you won't miss them. The trail stays in the dry wash for about 100 yards before it veers left (west) at the second park boundary sign.

For the next 7 miles, the trail stays in the broad valley. It's a well-defined, packed dirt trail all the way. It occasionally gets brushy as it weaves around the sagebrush, saltbrush, and rabbitbrush. In addition to watching deer bound away, you can see four beautiful arches—Kirk and Natural on your left, and Wedding Ring and Fisheye on your right. Kirk and Natural are on the skyline and easy to see, but only from a short section of trail so be alert. Wedding Ring is right by the trail, but surprisingly easy to miss, so watch carefully. Fisheye is very obvious, standing out right in front of you.

At the 3.5-mile mark, the vegetation changes dramatically. A large spring in the area has created a series of cattail marshes and willow thickets and, in a few places, patches of green grass. After emerging from the thickets, the spring flows over some flat rocks as a full-blown stream, a great place to relax for a while. There is a large pool below the spring, but please resist the temptation to jump in. All the springs in Upper Salt Creek provide critical water supplies to wildlife and backpackers. You could contaminate them with skin oils, sunscreen, or soap. Park regulations prohibit bathing in any water sources except the Colorado and Green rivers and in Salt Creek along the four-wheel-drive road.

About a quarter mile beyond the spring, you'll see Kirk Cabin and the remains of a ranching operation that predates the creation of Canyonlands National Park. This aging cabin is part of the cultural history of the park, so be careful not to artificially increase the rate of deterioration, just as you would be careful not to harm any ancient ruins or rock art.

Shortly after Kirk Cabin, the trail goes by the first backcountry campsites (SC1 and SC2) on the right (east) side of the trail. SC2 is about 100 yards from the trail nestled in a flat open spot in the sagebrush. SC1 is farther from the trail in a juniper stand and has a slightly better view. If you're on a two-night trip, one of these sites would be the best place to stop for the first night out.

.After Kirk Cabin, the trail continues to wind through the open valley floor. Keep your eyes peeled for arches in this section.

About a mile after Fisheye Arch, the trail goes by a famous rock art panel

A spring called "Upper Jump" in Upper Salt Creek.

called All American Man, perhaps because of its red, white, and blue pigments. Please don't climb up to the panel or touch this precious piece of art.

Right after All American Man, the trail goes through a narrow spot between two cliffs. It's almost like going through an arch, a big departure from the last five miles of open valley—a great place for a short rest and a good view of both where you've been and where you're going.

Shortly after this tight spot, you go though a big thicket with a noticeably flowing Salt Creek, which stays that way for most of the rest of the hike. Near the end of the thicket watch for Backcountry Campsite SC3 off to your left, a good choice for your second night out.

About a half-mile past the thicket, the trail passes a delightful spot where the stream falls over a rock ledge into a gorgeous pool. This is called Upper Jump, and it seems almost tropical and out-of-character for this neck of the woods. Again, please resist the temptation to jump into this critical water source.

After Upper Jump, the canyon walls gradually close in, and Upper Salt Creek starts to resemble many other canyons in the park. The trail also starts following the wide meanders of the stream. In fact, during the last 5 miles of the hike, the trail winds unmercifully. It seems to turn around every bush and crosses the stream dozens of times. The result is 5 miles of hiking to go about 2 miles "as the crow flies."

This section of trail also goes through several stretches of very thick brush. If you don't have long pants on, you might end up looking like a poster child for Neosporin. It's worth the time to stop and switch over to long pants.

In some places the trail stays on the bench above the stream and in other places it goes right into the brushy streambottom. When by the stream, it's nice and cool, and the trail is often carpeted with cottonwood leaves.

At the 12-mile mark, you'll see Backcountry Campsite SC4 on your right on a beautiful bench under some big cottonwoods, near the stream, and with a great view of a giant rock balanced on a sandstone spire. If you're out for three nights, this is your last chance to camp. It's only 1.5 miles to the Salt Creek Road from here.

When you reach an abandoned road, you might think this is the end of the trail, but not quite. You have to turn left onto the road and walk 0.2 mile more to the Salt Creek Road and the official trailhead for the Upper Salt Creek Trail.

Actually, at this point, you have one more option. If you have at least five days to spend in the wilderness, you can leave your vehicle at the Salt Creek gate and beg or bribe somebody to give you a ride to the Cathedral Butte Trailhead, you could now continue hiking down the Salt Creek Road for 13 more miles to the gate. At-large backpacking is allowed in Salt Creek Canyon and Horse Canyon, and there are many attractive campsites. But make sure to get a permit and camp at least a mile from the road and away from any water sources.

---

38   ANGEL ARCH

See Map on Page 118

Type of trail:	Out-and-back.
Type of trip:	Day hike.
Total distance:	1 mile.
Time required:	30-60 minutes.
Maps:	Trails Illustrated Needles and USGS Druid Arch.
Difficulty:	Easy.
Starting point:	Angel Arch Trailhead at the end of Salt Creek Road.

Finding the trailhead: From the entrance station, drive 0.9 mile and turn left (south) on a paved road marked Salt Creek. Follow this road for 0.5 mile, and then turn left (east) again on a gravel road which then turns right (south). Follow it for another 1.5 miles to the gate at the entrance to the Salt Creek Road. From here, use the combination on your permit to open the gate and follow Salt Creek Road) to the trailhead.

The hike: The trail starts right at the turnaround and parking area at the end of the Salt Creek Road. If you've been bumping and grinding for hours up the Salt Creek Road in your four-wheeler, a short hike up to Angel Arch with a picnic lunch probably sounds like a good idea.

The short, mostly level trail is easy to follow, but sandy most of the way. It climbs slightly near the end up to a small ridge that becomes a great viewing platform for this magnificent arch. However, the trail doesn't go all the way to the arch.

Type of trail:	Out-and-back.
Type of trip:	Day hike.
Total distance:	0.8 mile.
Time required:	30-60 minutes.
Maps:	Trails Illustrated Needles and USGS South Six-shooter Peak.
Difficulty:	Easy.
Starting point:	Castle Arch Trailhead near the end of the Horse Canyon Road.

Finding the trailhead: From the entrance station, drive 0.9 mile and turn left (south) on a paved road marked Salt Creek. Follow this road for 0.5 mile, and then turn left (east) again on a gravel road. Follow this as it turns right (south) and go for another 1.5 miles to the gate at the entrance to the Salt Creek Road. From here, use the combination on your permit to open the gate and follow Salt Creek Road and Horse Canyon Road to the trailhead.

ANGEL ARCH, CASTLE ARCH, FORTRESS ARCH

© National Geographic/Trails Illustrated

The hike: Just before the end of Horse Canyon Road, you'll see the trailhead sign for Castle Arch Trail and a spot to pull off the main road. From here, the trail heads west through a heavily vegetated valley.

This is a pleasant, slightly uphill hike. The trail is primitive and brushy in places, but nicely carpeted with oak leaves and a real treat for students of high desert vegetation. You can see the arch throughout most of the hike.

The trail doesn't go to the arch, and, in fact, has no clearly definable end. Instead, it just gets more and more faint, and you'll know when it's time to take one last look at Castle Arch and head back to your vehicle.

After you get back to your vehicle and if you're interested in more exercise, you can walk about a quarter-mile down the road to the Fortress Arch Trailhead and see both arches before getting back into your vehicle.

40   FORTRESS ARCH

<table>
<tr><td>Type of trail:</td><td>Out-and-back.</td><td rowspan="5">See Map on Page 118</td></tr>
<tr><td>Type of trip:</td><td>Day hike.</td></tr>
<tr><td>Total distance:</td><td>1 mile.</td></tr>
<tr><td>Time required:</td><td>30-60 minutes.</td></tr>
<tr><td>Maps:</td><td>Trails Illustrated Needles and USGS South Six-shooter Peak.</td></tr>
<tr><td>Difficulty:</td><td>Easy.</td></tr>
<tr><td>Starting point:</td><td>Fortress Arch Trailhead at the end of the Horse Canyon Road.</td></tr>
</table>

Finding the trailhead: From the entrance station, drive 0.9 mile and turn left (south) on a paved road marked Salt Creek. Follow this road for 0.5 mile, and then turn left (east) again on a gravel road. Follow this as it turns right (south) for another 1.5 miles to the gate at the entrance to the Salt Creek Road. From here, use the combination on your permit to open the gate and follow Salt Creek Road and then Horse Canyon to the trailhead at the end of Horse Canyon Road.

The hike: The Fortress Arch Trail starts right at the end of the Horse Canyon Road. From the parking area, it heads up a dry wash and stays there most of the way. It's easy walking all the way. The trail ends near a big, flat rock that makes an excellent spot to relax for a few minutes while you view this massive arch.

SQUAW FLAT TRAILHEAD

Finding the trailhead: To find the Squaw Flat Trailhead, go 40 miles south of Moab on U.S. Highway 191 and turn right (west) at the well-marked turn onto Utah 211 leading to The Needles District. Stay on this road for 34 miles until you reach the park boundary. Right after the entrance station, you'll see the Needles Visitor Center on your right (north). Keep going west for about 2.7 miles and turn left into Squaw Flat Campground. After entering the campground area, the road forks with both forks going to trailheads with access to the same trails. However, the left-hand fork takes you to the trailhead with the shortest access route to the backcountry. The right-hand fork and its respective trailhead are used mostly by campers staying in the campground.

41   PEEKABOO

<table>
<tr><td align="right">**Type of trail:**</td><td>Out-and-back.</td><td rowspan="2">See Map on Page 125</td></tr>
<tr><td align="right">**Type of trip:**</td><td>Long day hike or overnighter.</td></tr>
<tr><td align="right">**Total distance:**</td><td>10 miles (round-trip).</td></tr>
<tr><td align="right">**Time required:**</td><td>6-8 hours (round-trip).</td></tr>
<tr><td align="right">**Maps:**</td><td>Trails Illustrated Needles and USGS The Loop and Druid Arch.</td></tr>
<tr><td align="right">**Difficulty:**</td><td>Difficult.</td></tr>
<tr><td align="right">**Starting point:**</td><td>Squaw Flat Trailhead.</td></tr>
</table>

Key points:
      0.1   Junction with Squaw Canyon Trail.
      1.1   Junction with Peekaboo Trail.
      2.6   Junction with Lost Canyon Trail.
      5.0   Peekaboo Camp.

The hike: You have several options for seeing the Peekaboo Spring area. If you are in the mood for a long, strenuous day hike, it's 10 miles out-and-back. However, the Salt Creek Backcountry Road passes right by Peekaboo Camp, so you can have less ambitious members of your party meet you there for a quiet night in a beautiful desert campsite—if you can get a permit for this popular vehicle campsite. You can also make this an overnighter by camping at LC1 in Lost Canyon.

Immediately after leaving the trailhead, you reach the junction with the Big Spring Canyon Trail. Take a left here and head southeast toward Squaw Canyon.

The first 1.1 miles of the trail are flat and easy with the exception of several slickrock sections. The slickrock isn't dangerous, but be alert for small cairns marking the correct route. After 1.1 miles you hit another junction, also well signed. Take the left (east) fork toward Lost Canyon and Peekaboo Spring.

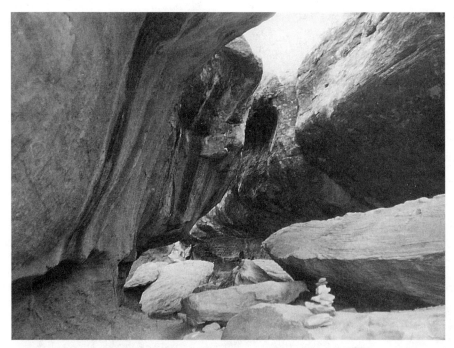

Just after leaving the Squaw Flat Trailhead, the Big Spring Canyon Trail passes through a narrow corridor of sandstone.

The next 1.5-mile section is gorgeous. It goes over slickrock for much of the first mile or so. Then, just after climbing down a small ladder, the trail follows the north rim of a beautiful, narrow canyon for a while before dropping into the sandy bottom of the canyon for the last half-mile or so to the junction with the Lost Canyon Trail. If you're staying overnight, LC1 is less than a quarter mile up the Peekaboo Trail on your right (south).

The Lost Canyon Trail junction is right in the dry wash of Lost Canyon. Go straight (east) across the wash instead of turning right (southwest) up Lost Canyon. Right after this junction, you quickly gain about 300 feet in elevation. This part of the hike is a bit rugged, but very scenic. In spring, the newly emerging leaves of the deciduous trees (oaks, cottonwoods, and willows) contrast nicely with the red and white sandstone formations in this area. Also, you're up on a ridgeline, so you can get great vistas in all directions. Near the end of the trail, you go right through a small arch, and several other small arches are visible.

Don't get too distracted by the scenery, though. You have to follow cairns most of the rest of the way to Peekaboo Camp.

Just before the end of the trail, you lose the elevation you gained coming out of Lost Canyon. It's steeper at the east end, and one spot could be dangerous if you aren't cautious. Fortunately, the NPS has installed a safety ladder to help you through this spot. After this steep section, it's about a

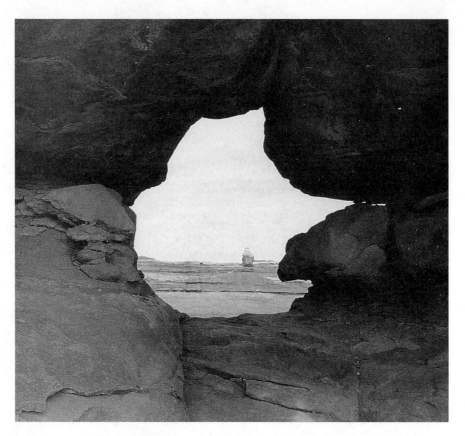

The Peekaboo Trail actually passes through a small, unnamed arch.

fourth-mile on a well-defined, flat trail along the streambed of Salt Creek to Peekaboo Camp, which is nicely located under some stately old cottonwoods.

After relaxing here for a while or staying overnight, retrace your steps to Squaw Flat Trailhead. While walking along Salt Creek (which often is flowing), be careful not to miss the trail when it takes a sharp left up a crack in the rock to reach the ladder you climbed down on your way to Peekaboo Camp.

42 LOST CANYON

See Map on Page 125

Type of trail:	Loop (actually a "lollipop").
Type of trip:	Long day hike or overnighter.
Total distance:	8.7 miles.
Time required:	5-7 hours.
Maps:	Trails Illustrated Needles and USGS The Loop and Druid Arch.
Difficulty:	Moderate.
Starting point:	Squaw Flat Trailhead.

Key points:

0.1	Junction with Squaw Canyon Trail.
1.1	Junction with Peekaboo Trail.
2.6	Junction with Lost Canyon Trail.
2.7	LC1 Backcountry Campsite.
3.8	LC2 Backcountry Campsite.
5.2	LC3 Backcountry Campsite.
5.4	Sharp right (south) turn in Lost Canyon Trail.
5.7	SQ2 Backcountry Campsite.
5.9	Junction with Squaw Canyon Trail.
6.7	SQ1 Backcountry Campsite.
7.6	Junction with Peekaboo Trail.
8.7	Squaw Flat Trailhead.

The hike: Lost Canyon is well named. It's not only the kind of place you could get lost in. It's also so beautiful that it is the kind of place you would *like* to get lost in. Like other loops, Lost Canyon can be done in either direction. This trail description describes the clockwise route.

The first 1.1 miles of the trail are the same as the Peekaboo (Hike 41) and Squaw Canyon/Big Spring Canyon (Hike 44) hikes. The trail is flat and easy with several slickrock sections. The slickrock isn't dangerous, but don't miss the sometimes-small cairns marking the correct route. The sandstone formations on the horizon along this section are marvelous.

After the first 1.1 miles of easy hiking, you reach the junction with the Peekaboo Spring Trail. Take a left (east) and head toward Lost Canyon and Peekaboo Spring.

The next 1.5-mile section is mostly slickrock. Just after climbing down a small ladder, the trail follows the north rim of a beautiful, narrow canyon for a short way before dropping into the canyon on a sandy trail for the last half-mile to the junction with the Lost Canyon Trail, which lies right in the dry wash of Lost Canyon. Take a right (southwest) here and start hiking up Lost Canyon. In spring, a healthy stream often flows through this lush canyon. If you're lucky enough to hike this after a rain, you actually might get your feet wet since the trail frequently crosses the streambed. But please don't wade in the water any more than necessary to cross the stream.

In spring, a live stream often follows the trail through Lost Canyon.

Lost Canyon starts out broad and flat, but gets narrow in places later on. The vegetation is more diverse than most other canyons in the area (to the point of getting brushy in a few spots), and there are no slickrock sections. The multi-hued vegetation contrasts beautifully with the reddish sandstone to create some fantastic scenery.

If you plan to stay overnight, Lost Canyon has three designated campsites, the first of which is on your right (south) just a few yards down the Peekaboo Trail. The second one is about a mile up the trail on your right, and the third site is on your right just as you start up a drainage back toward Squaw Canyon.

After hiking through Lost Canyon for about 2 miles, start watching carefully for a sharp turn to the right. There is a sign (pointing to "Lost Canyon Trail"), but if you're preoccupied with the scenery, you might miss it. An off-trail route continues up Lost Canyon, but at this point, the official trail leaves Lost Canyon and dips into a narrow, unnamed canyon that runs north to south. If you have extra time, you can take note of this spot, and then explore the upper reaches of Lost Canyon before heading back to the trailhead.

This slender, unnamed tributary is like a miniature Lost Canyon—smaller, but perhaps even more beautiful. After following the dry wash of the narrow gorge for about a half-mile, the trail climbs a steep chute (partly on an NPS-installed ladder) to a slickrock ledge. After cautiously hiking the ledge, you climb over a ridge. Then, follow a trail of cairns over slickrock for another half-mile or so until you drop into Squaw Canyon. This section can

© National Geographic/Trails Illustrated

be hazardous, so be careful, especially if you have children along. The junction is just after you cross the dry wash of Squaw Canyon.

If you didn't make your overnight stay in Lost Canyon, you have two more choices in Squaw Canyon. One site is on your left just before the junction with the Squaw Canyon Trail, and the second on your left is just less than a mile down the trail.

After hiking down Squaw Canyon for 1.7 miles you hit the Peekaboo Trail again, and then, you retrace your steps 1.1 miles back to the Squaw Flat Trailhead.

43 LOST CANYON/ELEPHANT CANYON

See Map on Page 125

Type of trail:	Loop.
Type of trip:	An overnighter (one or two nights).
Total distance:	13.8 miles.
Time required:	8-12 hours.
Maps:	Trails Illustrated Needles and USGS The Loop and Druid Arch.
Difficulty:	Moderate.
Starting point:	Squaw Flat Trailhead.

Key points:
- 0.1 Junction with Squaw Canyon Trail.
- 1.1 Junction with Peekaboo Trail.
- 2.6 Junction with Lost Canyon Trail.
- 2.7 LC1 Backcountry Campsite.
- 3.8 LC2 Backcountry Campsite.
- 5.2 LC3 Backcountry Campsite.
- 5.4 Sharp right (south) turn in Lost Canyon Trail.
- 5.7 SQ2 Backcountry Campsite.
- 5.9 Junction with Squaw Canyon Trail.
- 6.8 Junction with Big Spring Canyon Trail.
- 8.9 Junction with Druid Arch Trail.
- 9.0 UE1 Backcountry Campsite.
- 9.7 Junction with Chesler Park Trail.
- 0.3 Junction with the trail to Elephant Hill Trailhead.
- 12.6 Junction with Big Spring Canyon Trail.
- 13.8 Squaw Flat Trailhead.

The hike: If you can afford the time to make this a three-day trip, you will have the opportunity to see most of the outstanding features of the Needles area. A three-day trip provides the time for side trips to Peekaboo, Upper Lost Canyon, and Druid Arch without your overnight pack.

For no significant reason, this trail is described from a clockwise direction. It can be done quite pleasantly in either direction. In either case, however, be sure to take plenty of water and flashlights just in case you get caught out at night.

Slickrock section on the trail between Big Spring Canyon and Elephant Canyon.

The first 1.1 miles follow the same route as described in Peekaboo (Hike 41) and Squaw Canyon/Big Spring Canyon (Hike 44)—a flat and easy stretch of trail with several slickrock sections. Be alert not to miss the sometimes-small cairns marking the correct route over the slickrock.

After the first 1.1 miles of easy hiking, you reach the junction with the Peekaboo Spring Trail. Take a left (east) and head toward Lost Canyon and Peekaboo Spring. Most of the next 1.5-mile section is on slickrock. After climbing down a small ladder, the trail follows the north rim of a beautiful, narrow canyon for a short way before dropping into the canyon on a sandy trail for the last half-mile to the junction with the Lost Canyon Trail.

Take a right (southwest) here and start hiking up Lost Canyon. In spring, a healthy stream often flows through this lush canyon.

Lost Canyon starts out broad and flat, but gets narrow in places later on. It has more diverse vegetative growth than most canyons in the area. In a few spots, it actually gets brushy. The multi-hued vegetation of Lost Canyon contrasts beautifully with the reddish sandstone to create some fantastic scenery.

If you're spending two nights out, you might want to camp at LC1 or LC2 for your first night out. If you pick LC1 (on your right just past the Lost Canyon Junction at the 2.7-mile mark), you can set up camp and then conveniently hike over to Peekaboo Spring and return to camp.

You can also continue on to stay at LC2 (3.7-mile mark) or LC3 (5.2-mile mark). If you choose LC3, you will be conveniently located to spend your extra time exploring the upper reaches of Lost Canyon and then return to camp.

After hiking through Lost Canyon for about 2 miles, start watching carefully for an abrupt right-hand turn in the trail. There is a sign (pointing to "Lost Canyon Trail"), but if you're absorbed in the scenery, you might miss it. An off-trail route continues up Lost Canyon, but at this point, the official trail leaves Lost Canyon and dips into a narrow, unnamed canyon that runs north to south.

This small tributary is like a miniature Lost Canyon—smaller, but perhaps even more beautiful. After following the dry wash of the narrow gorge for about a half-mile, the trail climbs a steep chute to a slickrock ledge. After cautiously hiking the ledge, you climb over the ridge, then follow a trail of cairns over slickrock for another half-mile or so until you drop into Squaw Canyon. This section can be hazardous, so be careful. The junction is just after you cross the dry wash of Squaw Canyon.

Just before you reach the Squaw Canyon Trail, watch for Backcountry Campsite SQ2 on your left. If you're only taking two-days for this trip, this is probably your best choice for your overnight stay. However, staying out only one night results in two tough days and limits free time for side trips.

At the Squaw Canyon Trail junction, take a left and head southwest up Squaw Canyon. The trail quickly angles off to the right out of the canyon bottom onto slickrock. It stays on slickrock for most of the next 0.9-mile section to the junction with the Big Spring Canyon Trail. Take another left at this junction, continuing southwesterly, again mostly on slickrock, for 2.1 miles to the Druid Arch Trail. This is an especially scenic section of trail, and in one spot you climb over a slickrock pass with the help of a ladder on each side of a joint in the rocks.

Look for the sign at the end of this section of trail right in the dry wash of Upper Elephant Canyon. If you're staying two nights, you'll probably want to spend the second night at UE1 (on your right just south of the Druid Arch Trail at the 9-mile mark) or UE2 (on your right just down from UE1 on the Druid Arch Trail). Either site positions you nicely for a side trip that night or the next morning up to awesome Druid Arch.

When heading north down Upper Elephant Canyon, the trail follows the dry wash all the way. In a few places, you might not be able to see the trail, but don't fret. It stays right in the canyon bottom until you reach the Chesler Park Junction, and you can see strategically located cairns in most cases.

Turn right (east) at this junction. From here, the trail climbs out of Elephant Canyon. In 0.6 mile you see another junction with the left fork heading off to the Elephant Hill Trailhead. Unless you have arranged to leave a vehicle there (which would trim 2 miles off the hike), go right toward Squaw Flat.

The last 3.5 miles back to Squaw Flat alternate between flat sections with well-defined, sandy trails and small climbs over slickrock outcrops. At the 12.6-mile mark, you'll see the trail up Big Spring Canyon and Backcountry Campsite BS1 on your right, and then, near the end of the trail, the junction with the spur trail to the campground.

44   SQUAW CANYON/BIG SPRING CANYON

See Map on Page 125

Type of trail:	Loop.
Type of trip:	Day hike or overnighter.
Total distance:	7.5 miles.
Time required:	3-5 hours.
Maps:	Trails Illustrated Needles and USGS The Loop and Druid Arch.
Difficulty:	Moderate.
Starting point:	Squaw Flat Trailhead.

Key points:

0.1	Junction with Squaw Canyon Trail.
1.1	Junction with Peekaboo Trail.
2.0	SQ1 Backcountry Campsite.
2.8	Junction with Lost Canyon Trail.
3.7	Junction with Big Spring Canyon Trail.
5.3	BS2 Backcountry Campsite.
6.3	Junction with Chesler Park Trail.
6.4	BS1 Backcountry Campsite.
7.5	Squaw Flat Trailhead.

The hike: This might be the nicest, most accessible loop trail in all of Canyonlands National Park. It's nearly perfect for a moderate day hike to catch the essence of the Needles landscape, and since the NPS designated four backcountry campsites along this loop trail, it can also be an easy overnighter.

Immediately after leaving the trailhead, you hit the junction between Squaw Canyon and Big Spring Canyon trails. You can take the loop either way; one way is not noticeably more difficult than the other. This trail description takes the clockwise route because it makes two confusing spots in the trail easier to follow, so turn left (southeast) at this junction.

The next mile goes through fairly flat and open country (i.e., Squaw Flats) with scattered sections of slickrock. The slickrock sections aren't steep, but stay alert and follow small cairns showing the correct route.

When you reach the junction with the Peekaboo Trail, take a right (south) and head up Squaw Canyon. This leg of the loop trail follows Squaw Canyon, which often has a flowing stream in spring. Watch for Backcountry Campsite SQ1 on your right about a mile after the junction. If you've been lucky enough to time your hike while the stream has water in it, you'll probably be treated to a course of spadefoot toad music. Please do not wade in the water.

The canyon narrows in places just before you hit the junction with the Lost Canyon Trail at the 2.8-mile mark. If you cross the wash, SQ2 is down the trail about 100 yards on your right.

After this junction, get prepared for walking over slickrock. After a short section of well-defined, sandy trail along the streambed, the trail climbs up

The trail between Big Spring Canyon and Squaw Canyon.

on the north rim of the canyon and stays on slickrock all the way to the junction with the Elephant Canyon Spur Trail. This is a very scenic section, and a good place to have lunch if you're on a day hike.

At the junction with the Big Spring Canyon Trail, go straight and follow a string of cairns as you climb up a short but steep section to the top of a slickrock pass where you get a great view of the surrounding landscape. After soaking in the scenery, climb back down to the bottom of Big Spring Canyon. Even though the NPS has expertly plotted the easiest route over this slickrock pass, this section can be hazardous, especially when wet or with parties with children, so be careful.

After you get down into beautiful Big Spring Canyon, you might see some water flowing, especially in springtime. The canyon is narrow at this end but soon widens and stays that way until you get to the junction with the Elephant Canyon Cutoff Trail. Backcountry Campsite BS2 is on your left about 1.5 miles down the canyon. BS1 is right at the junction with the Elephant Canyon Cutoff Trail.

At this junction, keep going straight (north) and head toward Squaw Flats Trailhead. Here, the trail leaves Big Spring Canyon and heads across Squaw Flats. Just before you get to the trailhead, you'll see a trail going off to the left marked "Campground B." If you're staying at the B Loop of the campground, take a left, but if you started at the main trailhead, take a right. From this junction, it's only about a fourth-mile to the trailhead. The NPS has nicely routed the trail through some large boulders that in one spot look almost like a tunnel.

45 BIG SPRING CANYON/ELEPHANT CANYON

See Map on Page 125

Type of trail:	Loop (actually a "lollipop").
Type of trip:	Day hike or overnighter.
Total distance:	10.8 miles.
Time required:	5-7 hours.
Maps:	Trails Illustrated Needles and USGS The Loop and Druid Arch.
Difficulty:	Difficult.
Starting point:	Squaw Flat Campground.

Key points:

0.1	Junction with Squaw Canyon Trail.
1.2	Junction with Big Spring Canyon Trail.
2.2	BS2 Backcountry Campsite.
3.8	Junction with Elephant Canyon Trail.
5.9	Junction with Druid Arch Trail.
6.1	UE1 Backcountry Campsite.
6.7	Junction with Chesler Park Trail.
7.3	Junction with trail to Elephant Hill Trailhead.
9.6	Junction with Big Spring Canyon Trail.
9.7	BS1 Backcountry Campsite.
10.8	Squaw Flat Trailhead.

The hike: This hike is similar to the Squaw Canyon/Big Spring Canyon loop, but it's longer and slightly more rugged. If you aren't in good physical condition, it might be too much for a day hike. You can make it an overnighter by staying at one of several backcountry campsites along the way. You can follow the loop in either direction, but this trail description follows the clockwise route.

You immediately hit the Squaw Canyon/Big Spring Canyon Junction after leaving the trailhead. Take a right (south) and head toward Big Spring Canyon going through some large boulders just after the junction. Most of the first 1.2-mile section goes through flat, open country with many interesting sandstone features highlighting the horizon.

At 1.2 miles, you drop down into Big Spring Canyon, go by Backcountry Campsite BS1 on your left, and then see a junction with the trail up the canyon. If you're following the clockwise route, go straight (south) and head up this gorgeous desert canyon. In springtime, the stream is often flowing. The first part of Big Spring Canyon is wide open (watch for Backcountry Campsite BS2 slightly less than a mile after the junction), but the canyon narrows in the upper reaches.

At about the 2.8-mile mark, the trail abruptly leaves the canyon and angles off at about 30 degrees to the left, climbing up a slickrock pass along a string of cairns. Be alert so you don't miss this spot and continue up the canyon instead. From here, the trail makes a healthy climb for about a fourth-mile

Tight spot in trail between Big Spring Canyon and Elephant Canyon.

to the top of the pass where you get a great vista of the surrounding country. Then, the trail drops sharply down to the junction with the Elephant Canyon Spur Trail and Squaw Canyon Trail. You can see the sign from the top of the pass. The climb over the ridge has been plotted out nicely by the NPS but can be hazardous, so use caution.

At this junction, you turn right and head southwest on slickrock for most of the 2.1 miles to the Druid Arch Trail. This is an especially scenic section of trail, and in one spot you climb over a pass with the help of a ladder on each side of a joint in the rocks.

A sign marking the end of this section of trail is right in the dry wash of Upper Elephant Canyon. If you're ambitious, in good shape and you have enough daylight, you can take a left (south) and head up to Druid Arch for a scenic side trip. However, if you're following the loop trail, take a right (north) where the trail closely follows the dry wash. In a few places, you might not be able to see the trail, but it stays right in the canyon bottom until you reach the Chesler Park Junction.

Turn right (east) at this junction. Shortly thereafter, the trail climbs out of Elephant Canyon. In 0.6 mile you see another junction. The left fork goes to the Elephant Hill Trailhead. Unless you have arranged to leave a vehicle there (which would trim 2 miles off the hike), go right toward Squaw Flat.

The last 3.5 miles back to Squaw Flats alternate between flat sections with well-defined, sandy trails and small climbs over slickrock outcrops. At the 9.6-mile mark, you'll see the trail up Big Spring Canyon that you took earlier in the trip and shortly after that, Backcountry Campsite BS1 on your right. Then, near the end the trail, you'll cross the scenic boulder field you walked through at the start of your hike and return on the spur trail to the campground.

46 THE BIG NEEDLES LOOP

See Map on Page 125

Type of trail:	Loop.
Type of trip:	A multi-day backpacking trip (at least three nights out).
Total distance:	22 miles plus side trips.
Time required:	At least 4 days.
Maps:	Trails Illustrated Needles and USGS The Loop and Druid Arch.
Difficulty:	Difficult.
Starting point:	Squaw Flat Trailhead.

Key points:

0.1	Junction with Squaw Canyon Trail.
1.1	Junction with Peekaboo Trail.
2.6	Junction with Lost Canyon Trail.
2.7	LC1 Backcountry Campsite.
3.8	LC2 Backcountry Campsite.
5.2	LC3 Backcountry Campsite.
5.4	Sharp right (south) turn in Lost Canyon Trail.
5.7	SQ2 Backcountry Campsite.
5.9	Junction with Squaw Canyon Trail.
6.8	Junction with Big Spring Canyon Trail.
8.9	Junction with Druid Arch Trail.
9.4	Junction with Druid Arch West Trail.
10.4	Junction with Joint Trail.
10.5	CP2, CP3, CP4, and CP5 backcountry campsites.
11.1	Spur trail to Chesler Park Overlook and start of "joint."
11.9	Chesler Park Trailhead.
12.4	Junction with road to Beef Basin.
12.6	Trailhead for Devils Pocket Trail.
13.4	Junction with Chesler Park Loop Trail.
14.3	DP1 Backcountry Campsite.
14.8	Devils Kitchen Camp and Trailhead.
17.1	Junction with trail to Elephant Hill and Squaw Canyon.
17.9	Elephant Canyon dry wash, UE1 Backcountry Campsite, and junction with Druid Arch Trail.
18.5	Junction with trail to Elephant Hill Trailhead.
20.8	Junction with Big Spring Canyon Trail.
21.7	Junction with cutoff trail to Squaw Flat Campground.
22.0	Squaw Flat Trailhead.

The hike: The Needles Trails backcountry zone offers many opportunities for long backpacking trips, many of them without the problematic vehicle shuttle. The following description outlines one excellent route, but you can customize your own trip by studying the map and by changing or combining hikes outlined in this book.

Even though this trail description starts and ends at the Squaw Flat Trailhead, you could start or finish at three other trailheads (Elephant Hill, Devils Kitchen, or Chesler Park) and cover the same territory, but Squaw Flat is the most accessible trailhead and you can get there with any vehicle. This loop hike is one of the best because it has many interesting side trips such as Peekaboo Spring, Upper Lost Canyon, Druid Arch, Elephant Canyon, and Chesler Park Overlook.

The loop can be done in either direction with no real advantage or disadvantage, but this description follows the clockwise route. In any case, plan on a heavy pack, at least for the first two days, because of the amount of water you'll have to carry.

Deciding the length of your trip depends on how much water can you carry, how many miles can you cover in a day, and how much time you have available. This trail description covers the three-night/four-day option, but here's a quick summary of other options:

LENGTH OF TRIP	BACKCOUNTRY CAMPSITE	MILES PER DAY	SIDE TRIPS
Two-nights	1—SQ 2—DP1	1—5.7 miles 2—8.6 miles 3—7.7 miles	Upper Lost Canyon Chesler Park Overlook
Three nights	1—LC3 2—CP-2,3,4 or 5 3—DP1	1—5.2 miles 2—5.3 miles 3—3.8 miles 4—7.7 miles	Upper Lost Canyon Druid Arch Chesler Park Overlook
Four nights	1—LC1 2—LC3 3—CP-2,3,4 or 5 4—DP1	1—2.6 miles 2—2.6 miles 3—5.3 miles 4—3.8 miles 5—7.7 miles	Peekaboo Spring Upper Lost Canyon Druid Arch Chesler Park Overlook
Five nights	1—LC1 2—LC3 3—CP-2,3,4 or 5 4—DP1 5—ME1	1—2.6 miles 2—2.6 miles 3—5.3 miles 4—3.8 miles 5—3.6 miles 6—4.1 miles	Peekaboo Spring Upper Lost Canyon Druid Arch Chesler Park Overlook Elephant Canyon

NOTE: Be sure to get a map from the NPS showing exact locations of backcountry campsites.

The first 8.9 miles of this hike follow the same route described in Lost Canyon/Elephant Canyon (Hike 43), so refer to that description for details. Note the above chart for suggestions on backcountry campsites, and when you pick up your backcountry permit at the visitor center, be sure to get a map showing the location of backcountry campsites.

When going through Lost Canyon, watch carefully for an abrupt right-hand turn in the trail. There is a sign (pointing to "Squaw Canyon Trail"), but if you're absorbed in the scenery (which could easily happen), you might miss it. On the ground, the trail seems to continue into Upper Lost Canyon, but at this point, the official trail leaves Lost Canyon and dips into a narrow, unnamed canyon that runs north to south. If you have time, you might want to hike into Upper Lost Canyon on a side trip.

When you reach the Druid Arch Trail up Elephant Canyon at the 8.9-mile mark, you'll find the sign marking the junction right in the dry wash. Take a left and head toward Druid Arch instead of going right as you would if you were doing the Lost Canyon/Elephant Canyon hike (Hike 43).

After a 0.5-mile walk up Elephant Canyon, you'll see a junction with the trail going west to Chesler Park. If you're staying out for three or more nights, you probably have time to visit Druid Arch. If so, drop your pack somewhere around this trail junction and take a left for the scenic side trip up to awesome and well-named Druid Arch, as described in Hike 48.

When you get back to your pack, take the right fork (west) at this junction and go another mile to your camp at one of the four Chesler Park backcountry campsites. CP3, CP4, and CP5 are on your right just after you reach the junction with The Joint Trail, and CP2 is another 100 feet down the trail on your left. All four sites are nestled in the large boulders surrounding Chesler Park.

After enjoying your second night out on the rim of spectacular Chesler Park, keep heading west on The Joint Trail. In another 0.7 mile, you come to a junction where The Joint Trail drops down into the joint, and a side trail turns left to the Chesler Park Overlook.

If you want a short side trip, drop your pack here, perhaps grabbing a water bottle and a snack, and take this short trail up to the overlook. The side trail follows cairns for about a quarter-mile to the top of a slickrock ledge, a great place to relax for a while and soak in the quiet beauty of the Canyonlands. From here, you can see Chesler Park and the ring of sandstone spires that surround it. You've been able to see Chesler Park from your camp and from the trail, but the view is not nearly as dramatic as it is from this viewpoint.

After you return to your pack, head into the "joint"—a giant crack between rock formations that goes on and on, sometimes tight enough to make getting a big pack through difficult. Several trails in Canyonlands and Arches have similar joints, but this is, by far, the longest.

After about a quarter-mile of the joint, you finally break out into the sunlight again. From here, it's about a half-mile on a fairly rocky trail to the Chesler Park Trailhead where you'll find a vault toilet and picnic tables.

From here, walk down the road for 0.5 mile until you see the road to Beef Basin heading off to the left (south). You go right for another 0.3 mile until you see the Devils Pocket Trail veering off to the right.

The Devils Pocket Trail starts out through a flat, brushy meadow. After 0.8 mile, you'll see the Chesler Park Cutoff Trail going off to the right (east). Take a left, and make a fairly serious climb through a pass in the enormous Pinnacle Formation. After the pass, the trail drops into another dry, brush-covered flat, affectionately referred to as Devils Pocket.

In less than a half-mile, you'll see the short side trail to the DP1 backcountry campsite going off to the right. The campsite is about a quarter mile from the trail amid some large boulders and pinyon pine trees.

If you're out for three nights, DP1 is probably your best choice for a backcountry campsite. This leaves a tough 7.7 miles for the fourth and last day of your hike, but your pack will be its lightest on the last day as you deplete your water supply. (However, if you would like a short hike for the last day, you can go by DP1 and onto ME1, which would mean 7.4 miles of hiking on the third day but only 4.1 miles on the last day.)

After leaving DP1, it's only about a half-mile to Devils Kitchen Camp where you can find a vault toilet and picnic tables and four vehicle camp-sites. Some maps might not show it exactly this way, but the Devils Pocket Trail ends right on the road in Devils Kitchen and then heads out the east side of the vehicle camp. The trail out of Devils Kitchen is confusing. There are several unofficial trails made by visitors of the popular campground. Watch for the cairn-lined trail heading east from the vault toilet on the east end of the campsites. If there's any question in your mind, check the topo map and compass to make sure you don't have to backtrack to find the official trail. Note the Devils Pocket hike (Hike 53) for more details on this section of trail.

After hiking 2.8 miles from Devils Kitchen, turn left (east) on the trail to Elephant Hill Trailhead. On this short (0.6-mile) section of trail, you get fantastic views of the Pinnacle and the Needles before dropping into the dry wash of Elephant Canyon. From here, take a short trail north down the canyon to ME1 if you've decided to camp there.

If you're heading back to your vehicle, go across the dry wash on another 0.6-mile section of trail to a junction where you have a choice of trailheads. If your party had two vehicles, you may have left one at Elephant Hill Trailhead and cut 2.3 miles off your trip. If so, take a left (north) to Elephant Hill. If not, take a right (east) to Squaw Flat Trailhead.

ELEPHANT HILL TRAILHEAD

Finding the trailhead: From the entrance station, drive 3.1 miles on the main park road until you see a paved road going off to the left to Squaw Flat Campground and Elephant Hill. Take this left, and 0.3 mile later take a right on another paved road and then another right 0.5 mile later on the unpaved, two-wheel-drive Elephant Hill Access Road. Once on the unpaved road, it's 3 miles to the trailhead. Drive slowly on this road, especially around several blind corners.

47 ELEPHANT HILL TO SQUAW FLAT

See Map on Page 125

Type of hike:	Shuttle.
Type of trip:	Day hike.
Total distance:	5 miles.
Time required:	3-4 hours.
Maps:	Trails Illustrated Needles and USGS The Loop and Druid Arch.
Difficulty:	Moderate.
Starting point:	Elephant Hill Trailhead or Squaw Flat Trailhead.

Key points:

    1.5   Junction with trail to Squaw Flat Trailhead.
    3.8   Junction with Big Spring Canyon Trail.
    4.8   Cutoff Trail to Squaw Flat Campground.

The hike: If your party has two vehicles or you're staying at the Squaw Flat Campground and one member of your party volunteers to drop you off at Elephant Hill Trailhead, this is a great day hike.

Although the Needles District has a great variety of quality hiking opportunities, there aren't many hikes in the moderate, 5-mile range, so if that suits you, this trail is an excellent choice. You can do the shuttle in reverse, but this trail description starts at Elephant Hill Trailhead.

Right after leaving Elephant Hill Trailhead, the trail climbs a steep but short hill and then goes through a small joint between two rock formations. Then, the trail heads over a fairly flat stretch of slickrock with a good view of Big Spring Canyon off to the east and the Needles to the south.

At the 1.5-mile mark, you reach a junction with the Chesler Park Trail going to the right. Go left (east) and head toward Big Spring Canyon. This stretch of trail is pleasant walking as it alternates between well-defined packed dirt and short slickrock sections.

At the 3.8-mile mark, you'll see the Big Spring Canyon Trail coming in from the right and Backcountry Campsite BS1 straight ahead. If you want an easy backpacking trip, you could try to reserve this campsite and spend the night in the desert before covering the last 1.2 miles back to Squaw

Canyon Trailhead or Campground. If you're heading for the campground, watch for a signed cutoff trail going off to the left just before you reach the trailhead.

48 DRUID ARCH

See Map on Page 125

Type of hike: Out-and-back.
Type of trip: Long day hike or overnighter.
Total distance: 10.8 miles.
Time required: 6-7 hours.
Maps: Trails Illustrated Needles and USGS The Loop and Druid Arch.
Difficulty: Moderate.
Starting point: Elephant Hill Trailhead.

Key points:

1.5 Junction with trail to Squaw Flat Campground.
2.1 Junction with Druid Arch Trail.
2.2 ME1 Backcountry Campsite.
2.7 UE1 Backcountry Campsite.
2.9 Junction with trail to Squaw Canyon.
3.1 UE2 Backcountry Campsite.
3.4 Junction with trail to Chesler Park.
5.4 Druid Arch.

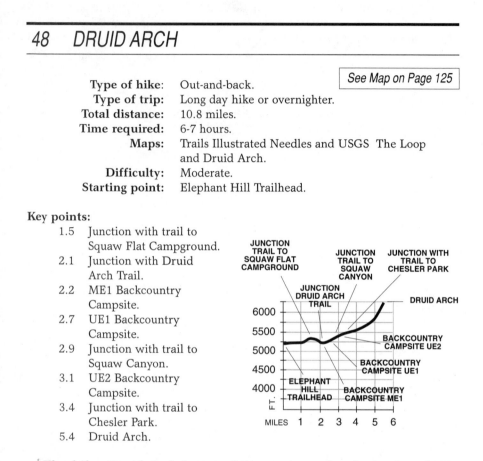

The hike: Druid Arch is one of the most popular destinations in the Needles District. In addition to seeing a spectacular arch, however, hikers can experience much of the special environment of the Needles area on the trail to the arch.

You can reach Druid Arch from several routes, including Druid Arch West (Hike 51) which offers a shorter route, but requires extra driving and a four-wheel-drive vehicle to reach the trailhead. However, the most commonly used route is the out-and-back route from Elephant Hill Trailhead.

Shortly after leaving the trailhead, you pass through a joint between two rock formations and then go over a stretch of slickrock before reaching the first junction at the 1.5-mile mark. The left fork goes to Squaw Flat Campground. You go right (west) on the trail to Chesler Park.

In the next short (0.6 mile) stretch of trail, you pass over the small divide between the Big Spring Canyon and Elephant Canyon. The trail goes through

Along the trail to Druid Arch.

a beautiful narrows where you get a good view both ways of these two canyons. Then, the trail drops into the dry wash of Elephant Canyon where you see the signs for Backcountry Campsite ME1 to the right (north) and Druid Arch to the left (south). Most hikers staying overnight choose UE1 or UE2 for their night out, but ME1 is also a great campsite located on a bench on the west side of the Elephant Canyon dry wash.

From this junction, the trail stays right in the Elephant Canyon dry wash. You'll see the trail to Squaw Canyon going off to the left (east). Keep going straight (south) up the canyon wash. You'll see UE1 and UE2 on your right less than a quarter mile up the trail.

Most of the last 2 miles of the trail to Druid Arch stays right in the dry wash of Elephant Canyon, sometimes leaving the canyon briefly on the left flank before dropping back into the dry wash again. Then, about a half-mile from Druid Arch, the trail starts climbing steeply up to a bench just below the well-named arch, a delightful place to spend an hour or two before retracing your steps to Elephant Hill Trailhead or your backcountry campsite.

49 CHESLER PARK/DEVILS KITCHEN

<table>
<tr><td>Type of hike:</td><td>Loop (actually a "lollipop").</td></tr>
<tr><td>Type of trip:</td><td>Overnighter.</td></tr>
<tr><td>Total distance:</td><td>13.9 miles.</td></tr>
<tr><td>Time required:</td><td>9-10 hours.</td></tr>
<tr><td>Maps:</td><td>Trails Illustrated Needles and USGS The Loop and Druid Arch.</td></tr>
<tr><td>Difficulty:</td><td>Moderate, but long.</td></tr>
<tr><td>Starting point:</td><td>Elephant Hill Trailhead.</td></tr>
</table>

See Map on Page 125

Key points:

1.5	Junction with Squaw Flat Trail.
2.1	Junction with Druid Arch Trail.
2.2	ME1 Backcountry Campsite.
2.7	UE1 Backcountry Campsite.
2.9	Junction with trail to Big Spring Canyon.
3.1	UE2 Backcountry Campsite.
3.4	Junction with side trail to Druid Arch.
4.4	Junction with Joint Trail.
4.5	CP2, CP3, CP4, and CP5 backcountry campsites.
4.8	Side trail to Chesler Park Overlook and start of the joint.
5.9	Chesler Park Trailhead.
6.4	Road to Beef Basin.
6.7	Devils Pocket Trailhead.
7.5	Chesler Park cutoff trail.
8.4	DP1 Backcountry Campsite.
8.9	Devils Kitchen Camp and Trailhead.
11.2	Junction with trail to Elephant Hill Trailhead.
11.8	Junction with Druid Arch Trail.
11.8	UE1 Backcountry Campsite.
12.4	Junction with Squaw Flat Trail.
13.9	Elephant Hill Trailhead.

The hike: This hike, like The Big Needles Loop (Hike 46), is the type of trip that can be crafted out of the Needles Trails Complex. Also like the Big Needles Loop, the trip can vary in number of nights out, can be taken clockwise or counterclockwise, and can start and finish at three different trailheads: Elephant Hill, Chesler Park, or Devils Kitchen. This description describes the clockwise route from the Elephant Hill Trailhead, but mainly because you can reach this trailhead with any vehicle. You need a high-clearance four-wheel-drive vehicle to get to Chesler Park or Devils Kitchen trailheads.

This long loop goes through a myriad of trail junctions, so keep your map out all the time and keep your bearings, lest you get on the wrong trail. It's fairly easy to get on the wrong trail with all the junctions and trails and canyons that can look alike.

This trip description covers the two-night option, but you can also do this one fairly easy in one night out or extend it to three. Here is a summary of options:

LENGTH OF TRIP	BACKCOUNTRY CAMPSITE	MILES PER DAY	SIDE TRIPS
One night	1—DP1	1—8.4 miles 2—5.5 miles	Chesler Park Overlook
Two nights	1—CP2,3,4, or 5 2—DP1	1—4.5 miles 2—3.9 miles 3—5.5 miles	Druid Arch Chesler Park Overlook
Three nights	1-CP2,3,4 or 5 2—same camp 3—DP1	1—4.5 miles 2—none. 3—3.9 miles 4—5.5 miles	Big Spring Canyon Druid Arch Chesler Park Overlook

NOTE: Be sure to get a map from the NPS showing exact locations of backcountry campsites.

Leaving Elephant Hill Trailhead, the trail starts out ominously, climbing a short but steep hill and then passing through a small joint between two rock formations. Then, the trail levels out for a pleasant half-mile walk on slickrock with expansive Big Spring Canyon off to the east and a good view of the Needles to the south.

At the first junction (at the 1.5-mile mark), take a right (west) and continue toward Chesler Park. The left trail goes over to Squaw Flat Campground. About a quarter-mile down the trail, you climb through a notch in the sandstone spires that is the divide between Big Spring Canyon and Elephant Canyon. Take a few minutes to enjoy the view both ways from the divide.

About a quarter mile later, you reach the next junction in the dry wash of Elephant Canyon. Take the sharp left (south) to Druid Arch which goes right up the dry wash. If you planned extra nights out and had a late start, you could stay at ME1, which is just off to the right about a quarter mile north on a scenic bench on the west rim of the dry wash.

Just past the junction with the trail going to Squaw Canyon, you'll see UE1 off to the right, another possible campsite for hikers who started late or wanted to have time to do the Druid Arch side trip on the first day out. Same goes for UE2, which is 0.2 mile past the junction with the trail going off to the left (east) to Squaw Canyon, another great side trip for hikers staying at UE1 or UE2.

At the 3.4-mile mark, you reach the side trail going up to Chesler Park. If you're camping in Chesler Park (an excellent choice for the second night

Hiking to Chesler Park from Elephant Hill Trailhead, the area's namesake; the Needles formation is in the background.

out) and have plenty of time you could stash your pack here and spend a couple of hours hiking to Druid Arch. For details refer to Hike 48.

To reach Chesler Park, take a right (west) at the Druid Arch junction, and go 1 mile to the junction with the Joint Trail on the southeast corner of Chesler Park.

If you're spending the night at Chesler Park (and you would be fortunate to have the opportunity) about 100 feet down the trail you'll first see the turn to the right to backcountry campsites CP3, CP4, and CP5. If you have a permit for CP2, it's another 50 feet down the trail on your left. All of these campsites could be described as a luxury suite in a five-star hotel. They're nestled in the huge sandstone boulders and spires surrounding Chesler Park, providing shade when needed and a great view out into the park. If you want to extend your trip from two nights to three nights, you might want to stay here two nights and spend the extra day taking short side trips from camp.

When you leave your camp in Chesler Park, head west on the Joint Trail for another 0.7 mile until you see a sign pointing to a side trail going left to the Chesler Park Overlook. Even though you've already seen Chesler Park, you get an especially grand view from this official overlook, so you would be wise to drop your pack and hike the short trail to the viewpoint. Being up here soaking in the wide sweeping vista is quite the contrast to the next leg of your trip, The Joint.

After you get your pack back on, you immediately drop down into the famed joint a seemingly endless section of trail that follows a long crack in the sandstone. In places, it gets difficult to fit an overstuffed backpack, but on a hot day, it's a welcome relief from the desert sun.

After about a quarter-mile in the joint, you finally break out into the sunlight again. From here, it's about a half-mile on a fairly rocky trail to the Chesler Park Trailhead where you'll find a vault toilet and picnic tables. From here, unfortunately, you have to take a short hike on a backcountry road. Walk down the road for 0.5 mile where you'll see the road to Beef Basin heading off to the left (south). Go right for another 0.3 mile until you see the Devils Pocket Trail veering off to the right. There is no sign right on the side of the road here. Instead, it's about 30 feet down the trail, so be sure not to miss the turn and keep walking down the road.

This trail starts out through a flat, brushy meadow. After 0.8 mile, you'll see the Chesler Park Cutoff Trail going off to the right (east). Take a left here, and make a fairly serious climb through a pass in the enormous Pinnacle Formation. After the pass, the trail drops into another dry, brush-covered flat called Devils Pocket.

Shortly thereafter, you'll see the short side trail to the DP1 backcountry campsite going off to the right. The campsite is about a quarter mile from the trail amid some large boulders and pinyon pine trees. This is your best choice for your second night out, leaving a moderate 5.5 miles for the third or fourth and last day of your hike.

After leaving DP1, it's only about a half-mile to Devils Kitchen Camp, where you can find a vault toilet and picnic tables and four vehicle campsites. The Devils Pocket Trail ends right at the road in Devils Kitchen and then heads out the east side of the vehicle camp. There are several unofficial trails made by visitors leaving this popular campground, so make sure you're on the right trail. Watch for the cairn-lined trail heading east near the vault toilet on the east end of the campsites. If there's any question in your mind, check the topo map and compass to make sure you don't have to backtrack to find the official trail. (Refer to Hike 53 for more details on this section of trail.)

After hiking 2.8 miles from Devils Kitchen, turn left (east) on the trail to Elephant Hill Trailhead. On this short (0.6-mile) section of trail, you get some fantastic views of the Pinnacle and the Needles before dropping into the dry wash of Elephant Canyon. From here, take a short trail north down the canyon to ME1 if you've decided to camp there.

If you're heading back to your vehicle, go across the dry wash on another 0.6-mile section of trail to the junction with the Squaw Flat Trail where you take a left (north) and go the final 1.5 miles back to Elephant Hill Trailhead.

DEVILS LANE TRAILHEADS

Finding the trailheads: From the Needles entrance station, go 13 miles east on Utah Highway 211 and turn right (south) on the Beef Basin/Elk Mountain Road. The sign at this junction parallels the road, so be careful not to miss it. If you're coming from Moab or Monticello, turn onto to Utah 211 and go 20.5 miles to the turnoff. From this junction, drive 42.8 miles to the park boundary. This road is passable for high-clearance two-wheel-drive vehicles when dry up to Cathedral Point. Beyond Cathedral Butte, the road becomes increasingly more difficult, requiring a four-wheel-drive vehicle, even in dry weather. However, rain or snow can make it impassable. There are a few stretches of clay that get extremely greasy when wet, and this can make the road impassable even for four-wheel-drive vehicles. The rangers at the Needles Visitor Center keep close track of these road conditions, so if there has been a recent rain, be sure to check with the NPS before heading up this road.

CHESLER PARK TRAILHEAD

Finding the trailhead: From the park boundary, take the four-wheel-drive road 4.7 miles into the park until you see the junction with the road to Chesler Park Trailhead. Turn right here and go 0.5 mile until the road deadends at the trailhead. Refer to Devils Lane (Road 14) for more details on road conditions. The trailhead has a vault toilet and picnic tables.

50   THE JOINT TRAIL

		See Map on Page 125
Type of hike:	Out-and-back.	
Type of trip:	Day hike.	
Total distance:	2 miles.	
Time required:	2-3 hours.	
Maps:	Trails Illustrated Needles and USGS Druid Arch.	
Difficulty:	Moderate.	
Starting point:	Chesler Park Trailhead.	

The hike: This is a most unusual hike, an excellent choice for those who want a little adventure (but not danger) and a hike that goes through some very interesting terrain (but not too long or too hard). The Joint Trail is just right for families with a four-wheel-drive vehicle. Getting to the trailhead is the hardest part of this trip.

The hike starts out uphill on a moderately rugged, rocky trail with cairns showing the way. In about a half-mile, it dips into a long, narrow joint between two rock formations. From here, it's like hiking in a very narrow slot canyon for about a quarter-mile. A few spots require a handhold to scramble over rocks in the joint, and near the end you climb manmade, but rustic, "stairs" just before you finally emerge from the depths of the joint.

Just as you break out into the daylight, you'll see a sign indicating a short viewpoint trail heading right (south) from the junction. The Chesler Park Trail veers off to the left (east). The viewpoint is only about a quarter mile from the sign, but it involves a short climb onto a slickrock ledge. This might be a little nerve-wracking for parents, but it's fairly safe. The steepest spots are made easier with little steps chipped out of the solid rock.

At the viewpoint, you get a fantastic view of Chesler Park—it's the perimeter of stately, multi-hued sandstone formations including the Pinnacle to the north. After soaking in the view and having a pleasant rest and perhaps lunch, it's back into the "underground" of The Joint again on the way back to the trailhead.

51 DRUID ARCH WEST

See Map on Page 125

Type of hike:	Out-and-back.
Type of trip:	Day hike or overnighter.
Total distance:	9 miles.
Time required:	6-8 hours.
Maps:	Trails Illustrated Needles and USGS Druid Arch.
Difficulty:	Moderate.
Starting point:	Chesler Park Trailhead.

Key points:
- 0.5 Start of The Joint.
- 0.8 Side trail to Chesler Park Viewpoint and end of The Joint.
- 1.4 CP2, CP3, CP4, and CP5 backcountry campsites.
- 1.5 Junction with Chesler Park Trail.
- 2.5 Junction with Druid Arch Trail.
- 4.5 Druid Arch.

The hike: The first part of this trail is described in The Joint Trail (Hike 50).

From the junction of the Chesler Park Viewpoint side trail, you hike east along the south edge of majestic Chesler Park. The trail is flat, packed dirt and well defined.

Just before you reach the junction with the trail going south to Chesler Park, you'll see Backcountry Campsite CP2 on your right and a short trail to CP3, CP4, and CP5 on your left. If you decided to make this a moderate overnighter, any of these scenic campsites would be your best choice. If you leave early enough, you can set up camp and still have time to hike to Druid Arch. If not (and perhaps even better) get up early the next morning to take the rest of the hike.

Just beyond the campsites, you'll reach a junction. Go right (east) here and head 1 mile down to the bottom of Upper Elephant Canyon where you'll see the Druid Arch Trail Junction in the canyon wash. Here, take a right (south) to Druid Arch.

The Druid Arch Trail alternates between the dry wash and short sections on the east flank of the canyon for about 1.5 miles until it climbs steeply up to a bench below Druid Arch. This is a great place to relax for a while before returning to your campsite or the trailhead.

Type of hike:	Loop.
Type of trip:	Day hike or overnighter.
Total distance:	4.9 miles.
Time required:	4-6 hours.
Maps:	Trails Illustrated Needles and USGS Druid Arch.
Difficulty:	Moderate.
Starting point:	Chesler Park Trailhead.

See Map on Page 125

Key points:
    0.5 Beef Basin Road Junction.
    0.8 Devils Pocket Trailhead.
    1.6 Junction with Chesler Park Cutoff Trail.
    2.8 Junction with Chesler Park Trail.
    3.4 CP1 Backcountry Campsite.
    4.1 Junction with Joint Trail.
    4.2 CP2, CP3, CP4, and CP5 backcountry campsites.
    4.8 Start of The Joint and Chesler Park Viewpoint trail junction.
    5.3 End of The Joint.
    5.8 Chesler Park Trailhead.

The hike: If you like to save the best until last, take this trail counter-clockwise. This involves walking on a road for the first 0.8 mile, but it's very easy going, and you're unlikely to see any vehicles.

The road forks 0.5 mile after leaving the trailhead with the left fork going off to Beef Basin. Take a right and walk another 0.3 mile until you see a sign for the Devils Pocket. The sign for this trail is not right along the road, so watch for it a few feet up the trail.

The next section of trail involves a gradual climb up to a junction with the trail through the Pinnacle to Devils Kitchen Camp. You go right (east) at this junction and head for Chesler Park, which is 1.2 miles to the east.

You go through one rocky section with one short, steep pitch before coming out into gorgeous Chesler Park, a huge grassy flatland ringed by colorful sandstone spires. The trail goes along the north edge of the park for less than 0.5 mile before hitting the next junction.

At this junction, turn right (south) and toward the Joint Trail. Follow the east edge of Chesler Park on a nicely defined and packed dirt trail for 1.3 miles to the next junction. Just less than halfway through this section, you'll see Backcountry Campsite CP1 on your left. It's back from the trail about 100 yards, out of sight between several large boulders, a great choice if you're staying overnight. It's shady and more private than the four camp-sites 0.7 mile down the trail.

When you reach the junction with the Elephant Canyon Cutoff Trail (which goes off to the east), go straight. In less than 10 yards, you'll see a side trail to Backcountry Campsites CP3, CP4, and CP5 off to your right and, a few steps down the trail, CP2 off to your left. CP2 and CP3 are fairly close to the trail, with CP3 having the best view of Chesler Park from camp. CP4 and CP5 are farther away from the main trail and more private.

All of the campsites are tucked amid gigantic boulders where you can always find shade. You'll also see some signs of historic ranching operations which operated in Chesler Park before the park was created.

From the campsites, the trail is flat and easy walking. Parts of this trail were, long ago, a primitive road. In 0.7 mile, you reach the start of The Joint and the side trail going to the left to the Chesler Park Overlook. Even though you've been walking through or on the edge of Chesler Park for a long time, you'll want to check out this viewpoint. It gives you a grand vista you don't get from the lower elevation trails. The viewpoint is only about a quarter mile off the main trail, and well worth the little climb up to a slickrock platform where you get a better-than-postcard panoramic vista of Chesler Park and the sandstone formations surrounding it.

Back at the viewpoint sign, the trail dives into The Joint, a large crack between rock formations. As you climb down manmade rock stairs to get to its depths, you might think you're not really on a trail, but you are. You stay in The Joint for another quarter mile. It's a tight squeeze in spots, but you shouldn't have any problems unless you're built like an NFL offensive lineman. However, you might have to push and twist to get a big backpack through The Joint.

After you come out into the sunlight again, it's about a 0.5 mile on a fairly rocky trail down to the Chesler Park Trailhead where you started the loop hike.

Chesler Park from the Chesler Park Overlook.

DEVILS KITCHEN TRAILHEAD

Finding the trailhead: Driving to Devils Kitchen Camp is only for people with high-clearance four-wheel-drive vehicles and experience using them. From the south boundary, drive north up Devils Lane Road for 4.7 miles to the junction with the Chesler Park Trailhead road. Continue straight (north) through the junction for another 3.1 miles, going over infamous SOB Hill until you see a junction with the Devils Kitchen Road. Turn right (east here) and go another 0.6 mile to Devils Kitchen Camp, where you'll find four premier vehicle campsites, a vault toilet, and picnic tables.

You can also reach Devils Kitchen from the north from the Elephant Hill Trailhead. The first 1.5 miles of this road go over Elephant Hill, technical four-wheel-driving most of the way. At the 1.5-mile mark, you'll see the one-way Cyclone Canyon road joining, but you can't turn right here. Continue straight on this road, which angles south, and in 2 miles you come to the Devils Kitchen side road. Turn left (east) here and go the last mile to Devils Kitchen Camp and Trailhead.

53 DEVILS POCKET LOOP

See Map on Page 125

Type of hike:	Loop.
Type of trip:	Day hike or overnighter.
Total distance:	5.1 miles.
Time required:	3-5 hours.
Maps:	Trails Illustrated Needles and USGS The Loop and Druid Arch.
Difficulty:	Moderate.
Starting point:	Devils Kitchen Trailhead.

Key points:
- 2.3   Junction with trail to Elephant Hill Trailhead.
- 2.5   Junction with Chesler Park Trail.
- 3.7   Junction with Devils Pocket Trail.
- 4.8   DP1 Backcountry Campsite.
- 5.1   Devils Kitchen Camp and Trailhead.

The hike: For somebody camped at Devils Kitchen, this is one of the two excellent choices for day hikes. The other is Lower Red Lake Canyon, which is longer and out-and-back as opposed to this delightful loop trail.

The loop can be taken from either direction, but the clockwise route is described here because it makes the climbs over the two passes through the Pinnacle slightly easier. This would be debatable, though. Either way will result in an enjoyable hike.

The trail starts just to the left of the sign at the south end of the camp-ground, and heads along a canyon wash for a few hundred yards and then

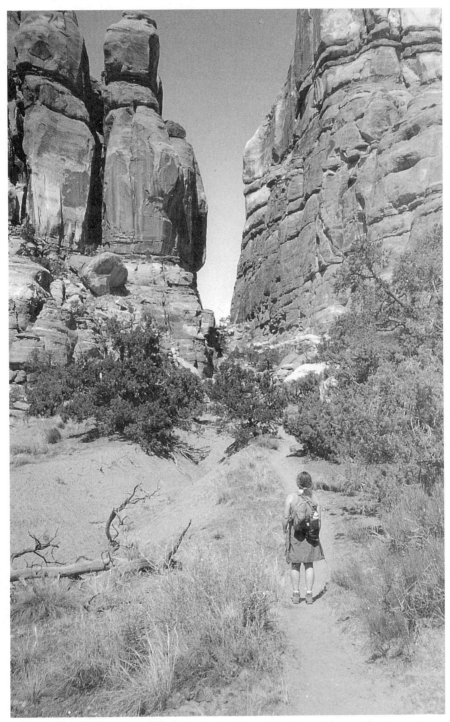

Hikers slip through a narrow pass in the Pinnacle Formation on their way to Chesler Park.

starts a gradual climb up toward the Pinnacle, a majestic sandstone formation and highlight of this section of the Canyonlands. The trail alternates between slickrock and well-defined dirt trail for the entire 2.3 miles to the junction with the Chesler Park Trail.

Take a right (southwest) at this junction. You'll quickly start a fairly serious, but short, climb to a narrow "pass" in the Pinnacle. At the top of the pass, pause to look both ways for an incredible view of Elephant Canyon (to the northeast) and Chesler Park (to the southwest). It's a very short section of trail, only 0.2 mile to the junction just downhill from the pass on the edge of Chesler Park. If you want to make this an overnighter, you should try to reserve Backcountry Campsite CP1, which is 0.6 mile south of this junction. The overnighter option will add about 1.2 miles to your trip.

From this junction, take a right (west) and walk on a packed dirt path along the north perimeter of Chesler Park for about a half mile before heading down a rocky section toward the next junction. Here, take another right (north) and start climbing up to the second pass through the Pinnacle.

After descending from the pass, the trail goes through a series of open parks, mostly on packed dirt with a few stretches of loose sand. Less than a half-mile from Devils Kitchen, you'll see Backcountry Campsite DP1 on your right. This is an adorable site about 100 yards off the trail and nestled between two big boulders under some pinyon pines.

The rest of the trail is flat on loose sand until you come back to Devils Kitchen right by the sign where you started.

54   LOWER RED LAKE

Type of hike:	Out-and-back.
Type of trip:	Day hike or overnighter.
Total distance:	11 miles.
Time required:	7-10 hours.
Maps:	Trails Illustrated Needles and USGS The Loop and Spanish Bottom.
Difficulty:	Difficult.
Starting point:	Devils Kitchen Trailhead.

Key points:
- 1.0   Devils Lane Road
- 1.9   Cyclone Canyon Road.
- 2.7   Lower Red Canyon.
- 4.0   Lens Canyon.
- 5.9   Colorado River.

LOWER RED LAKE

© National Geographic/Trails Illustrated

The hike: This is a long, hot, steep trail, but it goes into one of the most remote and little used sections of Canyonlands National Park. You stand a good chance of having the trail all to yourself.

From Devils Kitchen Camp, you can drive about 0.6 mile to the junction with the Devils Lane Road where you'll see the trailhead for the Lower Red Lake Trail going straight off to the west. However, there is no parking area at the trailhead, so it's best to leave your vehicle in Devils Kitchen Camp and hike from there.

From the trailhead, the trail goes over a small ridge for 0.9 mile to the recently abandoned Cyclone Canyon Road. This is easy walking on a well-defined trail. Until 1996, hikers could cut this first mile off the trip by driving around the Cyclone Canyon Road to this point, but the NPS is converting the last stretch of the Cyclone Canyon Road to a trail.

Once across the road, the trail starts getting rougher and rougher as it drops into Red Lake Canyon. This is the start of an 800-foot descent to the Colorado River.

Once at the bottom of Red Lake Canyon, the trail angles off to the right and more or less stays in the canyon bottom the rest of the way to the river. Less than a half mile down the trail, it turns left toward the river. A mile or so later, you'll see impressive Lens Canyon joining from the north. Lower Red Lake Canyon is steep-walled and rugged the rest of the way.

The terrain flattens out somewhat when you reach the river, but regrettably, the area has been burned and invaded by the evil Tamarisk which now dominate the river bank.

You can camp at-large along Lower Red Lake Canyon, but in this steep canyon it's difficult to find a good campsite. If you're on a long day hike, take a long rest at the river. It's a steep climb back up to Devils Kitchen.

BACKCOUNTRY ROADS

9 SALT CREEK

Starting point:	Salt Creek Trailhead at locked gate.
Finding the trailhead:	Drive 0.9 mile west from the entrance station and take a left (south) on a well-signed, paved road (marked Salt Creek) and go 0.5 mile before taking a left (east) on a two-wheel-drive unpaved road. About 0.5 mile up the unpaved road, turn right (south) instead of going straight to the Cave Spring Trailhead. Then, go 0.5 mile more until you see a locked gate across the road. This gate marks the official trailhead for the Salt Creek and Horse Canyon roads.
Total distance:	From the locked gate, it's 14 miles (one way) to the end of the road.
Key points:	2.3 Junction with Horse Canyon Road.
	3.3 Peekaboo Camp.
	13.0 Upper Salt Creek Trailhead.
	14.0 Angel Arch Trailhead and end of Salt Creek Road.
Time required:	5-7 hours (round trip), not including side trip to Horse Canyon or any hiking.
Maps:	Trails Illustrated Needles and USGS The Loop, South Six-shooter Peak and Druid Arch.
Permits:	The first step on your trip to Salt Creek is a stop at the Needles Visitor Center to get a permit. You need a permit for overnight or day use. Salt Creek has only two vehicle campsites (both at Peekaboo Camp), so overnight permits are often difficult to get. To improve your chances, use the park's reservation system. You can reserve a day-use permit in advance just like you do overnight permits. If you feel lucky, you can take a chance and simply go to the visitor center and hope all permits aren't taken for that day. If you want to get a day-use permit when you get to the Needles, try to get to the visitor center early in the day. When you get your permit, a ranger gives you the combination (changed daily) to the locked gate at the trailhead. Listen carefully on how to use the combination lock. It can be tricky.
Minimum vehicle requirements:	High-clearance four-wheel-drive.
Difficulty:	Moderate.
Road conditions:	The first 2.5 miles are the most difficult part of the road because you pass through several sections of

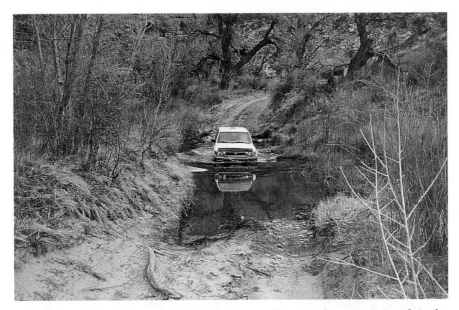

The Salt Creek Road crosses Salt Creek many times on the way to Angel Arch.

very loose sand where you must keep your speed up. The rest of the road is easy going with the exception of frequent stream crossings. In spring, some of the water stretches can go on for 100 yards or more. At about the 11-mile mark, the road goes through a short section of slickrock with a few small ledges, but it can be safely driven at very low speeds.

Suitability for mountain biking:	The NPS does not recommend mountain biking in Salt Creek. Loose sand in the first 2.5 miles and frequent stream crossings all along the road would make mountain biking marginal at best.
Hiking:	From Peekaboo Camp, you can hike east up the Peekaboo Trail (Hike 41) toward Lost Canyon. You can also hike down the road north or south from the campsite. At the end of the Salt Creek Road, you can hike into Angel Arch (Hike 38) or Upper Salt Creek (Hike 37).
Vehicle camps:	Peekaboo Camp (two campsites) is on your right about a mile after the junction with the Horse Canyon Road. It's a lovely site under some huge cottonwood trees but quite close to the road, making privacy during midday difficult.
Special attractions:	Besides being a gorgeous high desert canyon, Salt Creek attracted many early residents, mainly because of the reliable water sources it offered. As a

result, the canyon has numerous ruins and rock art panels.

Special precautions: Salt Creek is subject to flash floods. To be safe, take sleeping bags; water filter, water purification tablets, or extra water; and emergency food for two or three days. And, of course, keep your eye on the weather conditions.

BE OBSERVANT

A wealth of rock art panels lies hidden in the overhanging cliffs and high alcoves of Salt Creek and Horse Canyon. Mainly because of the reliable water sources, Archaic and ancestral Puébloan Indians inhabited this area over a span of at least two hundred years. These early residents used the area extensively for farming, which explains the large number of granaries found in the canyon.

The National Park Service has designated the area The Salt Creek Archeological District. In 1975, the district was placed on the National Register of Historic Places. Be extremely careful not to disturb any ruins, granaries or rock art. If you observe anybody else disturbing these fragile resources, please report it to a ranger.

---

10 HORSE CANYON

Starting point: Salt Creek Trailhead at the locked gate.

Finding the trailhead: Refer to Road 9, Salt Creek.

Total distance: From the locked gate, it's 7 miles (one way) to the end of the road, plus the 0.5-mile (one way) road to the Tower Ruin Viewpoint.

Key points:
2.5   Junction with Salt Creek Road.
3.5   Paul Bunyan's Potty.
4.5   Tower Ruin Road.
8.5   Castle Arch Trailhead.
8.7   Fortress Arch Trailhead and end of Horse Canyon Road.

Time required: 2-3 hours, not including 1-mile (round-trip) to Tower Ruin Viewpoint or any hiking. If you want to drive to the end of the road, take the spur road to Tower Ruin, stop and see Paul Bunyan's Potty, and take the short hikes to Castle and Fortress arches, set aside an extra half-day.

Maps: Trails Illustrated Needles and USGS The Loop, North Six-shooter Peak, and South Six-shooter Peak.

Permits:	Overnight and day use permits required. Check at the Needles Visitor Center, and refer to Road 9, Salt Creek.
Minimum vehicle requirements:	High-clearance four-wheel-drive.
Difficulty:	Moderate.
Road conditions:	Although Horse Canyon is, for the most part, easy four-wheeling, you must go through the first 2.5 miles of Salt Creek to get there. This section has several sections of loose sand where you must keep your speed up. Just before the Castle Arch Trailhead, there's one tight spot between a boulder and a cliff where you could leave some paint on a rock if you aren't careful.
Suitability for mountain biking:	The NPS does not recommend mountain biking in Horse Canyon. Some parts of Horse Canyon would be fair mountain biking, but several stretches of loose sand would be difficult. Getting through the first 2.5 miles of Salt Creek would make the area marginal at best for mountain biking.
Hiking:	At the end of the road, you can take two short hikes to Castle Arch and Fortress Arch. Refer to Hikes 39 and 40. You might want to leave your vehicle at Castle Arch trailhead and hike both to Castle and Fortress from there instead of driving the last quarter mile. It's probably easier and faster to walk.
Vehicle campsites:	No vehicle campsites, but the parking area for Paul Bunyan's Potty has a vault toilet.
Special attractions:	Paul Bunyan's Potty is an unusual (but well-named) pothole arch. Also, be sure to take the spur road to see Tower Ruin, among the most spectacular anywhere. It's in an alcove high above the valley floor. Don't climb up to this fragile site. Instead, just look and marvel about what it must have been like to build it, get water up there, or even live there.

11 COLORADO OVERLOOK

Starting point:	Needles Visitor Center.
Finding the trailhead:	The visitor center is on your right (north) 0.9 mile past the entrance station.
Total distance:	From the visitor center, it's 7 miles (one way) to the overlook parking area.
Time required:	2-3 hours.
Maps:	Trails Illustrated Needles and USGS The Loop.
Permits:	No permit required.

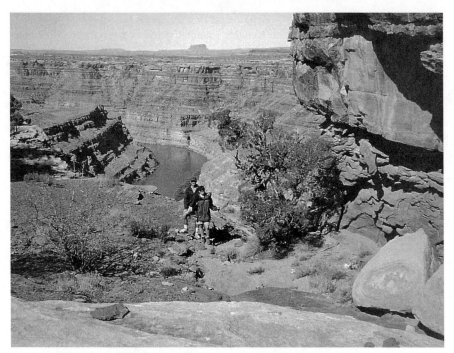

At the end of the Colorado Overlook Road with the Colorado River in the background.

Minimum vehicle requirements:	High-clearance four-wheel-drive.
Difficulty:	Moderate.
Road conditions:	First 3 miles are on packed dirt and easily passable with a two-wheel-drive vehicle. Then, the road gets rocky as it goes over several slickrock sections. The last mile is the toughest—it's mostly slickrock with several significant ledges.
Suitability for mountain biking:	Excellent mountain biking.
Hiking:	When you get to the end of the road, you might want to carefully hike around the point that separates the Colorado River on your right and Salt Creek on your left.
Vehicle campsites:	No vehicle campsites.
Special attractions:	Note the incredible canyon gouged out by Salt Creek on its way to the Colorado River.
Special precautions:	This is an unfenced overlook with very steep cliffs, so be careful not to get too close to the edge. Keep the kids by your side.

12 LAVENDER CANYON

Starting point:	Locked gate at park boundary.
Finding the trailhead:	From the Needles entrance station, drive 7.6 miles east on Utah Highway 211 and turn right (south) at a road marked "Davis Canyon." If you're coming from the other direction, this turn is 25.9 miles from U.S. 191. After turning off Utah 211, drive 13.9 miles on an unpaved road to the park boundary. The first 3 miles have a few rocky spots. Then, at the 3-mile mark, you see a road going off to the right up a dry wash. It's tempting to take that road, but it doesn't go to Lavender Canyon. Go across the dry wash, staying on the road you're driving. There should be a sign indicating Lavender Canyon to the left. A mile or so after the sign, you drop down into Lavender Canyon, and the road turns (south) and heads up the dry wash and stays there all the way to the park boundary.
Total distance:	From Utah 211, it's 13.9 miles (one way) to the park boundary. From the park boundary, it's 4.1 miles (one way) to the end of the main road or 3 miles (one way) to end of the west fork road of the West Fork of Lavender Canyon.
Key points:	0.1 First gate.
	0.7 Left turn at an unsigned junction.
	0.8 Wooden gate.
	3.0 Right turn at a signed junction.
	13.9 Locked gate at park boundary.
	14.4 Split in road.
	17.4 Cleft Arch.
	18.0 End of main road.
Time required:	7-9 hours to see both canyons, not including any hiking.
Maps:	Trails Illustrated Needles and USGS South Six-shooter Peak and Hans Point.
Permits:	Day use permit required, available at the Needles Visitor Center. At the park boundary, you'll find a locked gate and that opens with the combination the ranger writes on your permit. The combination changes every day, so you must come in and out on the days designated on the permit.
Minimum vehicle requirements:	High-clearance four-wheel-drive.
Difficulty:	Moderate.
Road conditions:	The condition on the unpaved road to the park boundary is good. Inside the park, the roads are mostly packed dirt with frequent sections of loose sand and a few short rocky sections. The road up the West Fork of Lavender Canyon (not shown on some

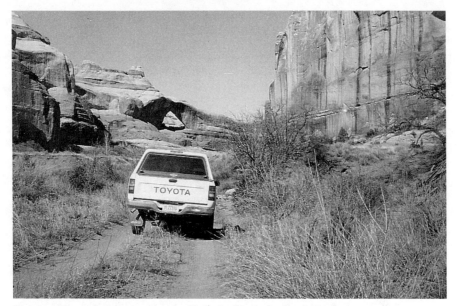

Driving Lavender Canyon with Cleft Arch on the horizon.

maps) is more narrow and difficult than the main road. Some maps show the main road splitting again near the end of the road, but the righthand road only goes about 100 yards from the main road.

Suitability for mountain biking: Difficult mountain biking (both inside and outside the park) because of the abundance of loose sand.

Hiking: When you reach the end of the main road or the west fork road, you can hike up the canyon for a short way.

Vehicle campsites: No vehicle camping allowed in Lavender Canyon. At-large backpacking with a permit is allowed, but you must leave your vehicle at the park boundary.

Special attractions: Under the right light conditions, the canyon walls such as those to the east dropping down from Bridger Jack Mesa really do get a beautiful lavender color. In the first half-mile after entering the park, watch for two beautiful, but easy-to-miss, arches on the western rim of the canyon. The first is Natural Arch. About 200 yards later, you can see the second, Caterpillar Arch. Most maps note only one or the other of these two arches, but not both. Cleft Arch at the end of the main road is also an awesome sight.

Special precautions: The road to the park boundary goes through ranching operations on private land and through leased BLM land, so watch carefully for cattle (especially in spring when calves are running around carefree) and respect private property in the area. Be sure to close all gates behind you.

13 DEVILS LANE/CONFLUENCE OVERLOOK

Starting point: Park boundary.

Finding the trailhead: From Utah 211, drive 42.8 miles to the park boundary, staying on the main Elk Mountain/Beef Basin Road all the way.

Total distance: From Utah 211, it's 42.8 miles (one way) to the park boundary. From the park boundary, it's 12.3 miles (one way) from park boundary to the Confluence Overlook Trailhead.

Key points:
0.5	South boundary Hill (short rocky section).
3.8	Road to Bobby Jo and Horsehoof camps.
4.7	Road to Chesler Park Trailhead.
5.0	Devils Pocket Trailhead.
6.6	SOB Hill.
7.8	Road to Devils Kitchen Camp, Lower Red Lake Trailhead.
8.4	Silver Stairs.
8.7	One way road to Elephant Hill.
9.1	New Bates Wilson Camp.
11.4	Confluence Overlook foot trail.
12.0	Junction with roads to Confluence Overlook (west) and Cyclone Canyon Trail.
12.3	Confluence Overlook Trailhead.

Time required: 2-3 hours (one way) from Utah 211 to the park boundary (on dry roads), plus 5-6 hours (one way) to the Confluence Overlook Trailhead.

Maps: Trails Illustrated Needles and USGS Cross Canyon, Spanish Bottom, Druid Arch, and The Loop.

Permits: No permit necessary for day use, but overnight vehicle camping or at-large backpacking permits required.

Minimum vehicle requirements: High-clearance four-wheel-drive.

Difficulty: Difficult.

Road conditions: With the exception of three technically difficult sections (South Boundary Hill, SOB Hill, and Silver Stairs), the road is easy four-wheeling, mostly packed dirt with a few short rocky sections and some loose sand.

Suitability for mountain biking: Moderate mountain biking with a few sections of loose sand.

Hiking:	Numerous hiking opportunities from trailheads at Chesler Park and Devils Kitchen. (Refer to Hikes 36 and 50-54.) Most visitors at least take the 0.5-mile hike into the Confluence Overlook (Hike 36) from the end of the road.
Vehicle campsites:	Bobby Jo (two campsites), Horsehoof (one campsite), and New Bates Wilson Camp (two campsites).
Special attractions:	Confluence Overlook and challenging sections for experienced four-wheelers.
Special precautions:	The Confluence Overlook is unfenced, so please be careful, especially with kids.

14 ELEPHANT HILL/DEVILS POCKET LOOP

Starting point:	Elephant Hill Trailhead.
Finding the trailhead:	From the entrance station, drive 3.1 miles on the main park road until you see a paved road going off to the left to Squaw Flat Campground and Elephant Hill. Take this left and then 0.3 mile later take a right on another paved road. Take another right 0.5 mile later on the unpaved, two-wheel-drive Elephant Hill Road. Once on the unpaved road, it's 3 miles to the trailhead. Drive slowly on this road, especially around several blind corners.
Total distance:	9.4 miles.
Key points:	1.5 Junction with one-way road.
	3.5 Devils Kitchen Camp, Devils Pocket Trailhead.
	4.5 Junction with Devils Lane Road, Lower Red Lake Trailhead.
	5.1 Silver Stairs.
	6.1 Junction with one-way road.
	8.3 Junction with Elephant Hill Road.
	9.4 Elephant Hill Trailhead.
Time required:	5-7 hours.
Maps:	Trails Illustrated Needles and USGS The Loop.
Permits:	No permit required for day use. Permits required for vehicle camping or at-large backpacking.
Minimum vehicle requirements:	High-clearance four-wheel-drive.
Difficulty:	Difficult.
Road conditions:	Starting right at the trailhead, Elephant Hill is extremely technical four-wheeling, as is the Silver Stairs section about halfway around the loop. Plus, there are a few more difficult sections. Between these rocky, technical spots, however, the road is easy driving on packed dirt with some loose sand. Keep in mind that this one-way loop can only be done in a clockwise direction.

160

<table>
<tr><td align="right">**Suitability for
mountain biking:**</td><td>Fair to good with slow going in technical sections over Elephant Hill and Silver Stairs and through some short sections of loose sand.</td></tr>
<tr><td align="right">**Hiking:**</td><td>From Devils Kitchen Camp, try the Pinnacle Loop (Hike 53) or Lower Red Lake (Hike 54).</td></tr>
<tr><td align="right">**Vehicle campsites:**</td><td>Devils Kitchen (four campsites), nestled amid large boulders and narrow spots between rock formations.</td></tr>
<tr><td align="right">**Special attractions:**</td><td>Definitely challenging for the experienced four-wheeler.</td></tr>
<tr><td align="right">**Special precautions:**</td><td>Be sure to check which sections of the loop are one-way travel only.</td></tr>
</table>

THE MAZE, ORANGE CLIFFS AND HORSESHOE CANYON

OVERVIEW

When somebody uses the old adage "in the middle of nowhere," they could easily be talking about the Maze, and it would be a compliment.

Most people have never been to a place as remote as the Maze, and getting there can be a great warm-up for experiencing this remote district on Canyonlands National Park. Whether you come from Hite, Hanksville, or Green River, you definitely get the feeling of being out of touch with civilization long before you reach the park boundary. Once you start slowly maneuvering your vehicle up the primitive roads into the Maze, you complete the feeling of being totally self-reliant. The allure of extreme remoteness experienced in the Maze can't be found in most national parks.

Self-reliance is the undertone of the management policy of the Maze District. This network of twisted sandstone canyons is for rugged individuals who can take care of themselves and their vehicle. There's no gas station or restaurant food or room service for 50-plus miles in any direction. And even those 50 miles don't tell the true story because it might take a half-day to cover that distance on these roads.

In many national parks, including other sections of Canyonlands, the NPS provides great "customer service." But not in the Maze. The Maze District of Canyonlands National Park combined with the Orange Cliffs Unit of Glen Canyon National Recreation Area (NRA) is larger than many national parks, but once you leave the Hans Flat Ranger Station, there are no services provided, no guided tours, no facilities, no toilets, not even an entrance station. You are on your own.

In the Maze District, you should measure roads and trails in hours instead of miles. A 1-mile trail or a 5-mile stretch of road can take 3 hours to hike or drive. Under any circumstances, don't be in a hurry.

THE MAZE

To
Green River

Green River

GLEN
CANYON
NATIONAL
RECREATION
AREA

Hans Flat

THE MAZE

Colorado River

To
Hyte

CANYONLANDS
Island in the Sky

GLEN
CANYON
NRA

NATIONAL

The Maze

PARK

Needles

LEGEND

🛡70 Interstate	▭▭▭	Interstate Highway
191 U.S. Highway	▭▬▭	Paved Road
211 State or Other Principal Road	▬▬▬	Unpaved Road
	====	4-wheel-drive Road

After a heavy rain, the clay coating on some roads in the Maze (particularly the Flint Trail) makes them too slippery to drive. Also, in winter months, ice and snow can make the roads impassable. During the winter, the Flint Trail is usually closed.

Before you go to the Maze District, make sure you know where you're going, what to bring, and how to prepare. This isn't like going to other national parks. If you show up without the necessary gear to survive on your own, you won't enjoy the Maze District—and probably should not try to. Yet, it happens all the time. People show up in a standard rental car that's not supposed to be driven off paved roads, and they expect to get into the Maze. This is a bad idea!

GETTING THERE

From Hanksville, go north 21 miles on Utah Highway 24 and turn right (east) on a major unpaved, two-wheel-drive road marked with signs for the Glen Canyon National Recreation Area and Canyonlands National Park. From here, it's 46 miles to Hans Flat Ranger Station with right-hand turns at the 11-mile mark and the 24-mile mark, both junctions well-signed.

From the Hite Marina on Lake Powell, take Utah Highway 95 north 2 miles and turn right (east) on an unpaved two-wheel-drive road. From here, it's about 59 miles to the Hans Flat Ranger Station with several junctions once you get to the park, all well signed.

From Green River, go to the middle of town and watch for Long Street. Turn south on Long Street and follow it to the edge of town, following the signs to the Airport. The road stays paved until it passes under Interstate 70 and turns into an unpaved two-wheel-drive road. It stays that way for 68 miles to Hans Flat Ranger Station. At the 28-mile mark, take a left at the junction with the Dugout Spring Road and, at the 46-mile-mark, take another left at the Hanksville junction.

If you want to see Horseshoe Canyon (and you'll be missing something if you don't), watch for a small sign at the 41-mile mark that says "Horseshoe Canyon Foot Trail 2 Miles." If you hit the junction with the road from Hanksville, you've gone about 5 miles too far. If you're coming from Hanksville, take a left at the same junction and go 5 miles north.

SPECIAL REGULATIONS FOR THE MAZE

In addition to park regulations listed on page 15, the NPS has a few special rules for the Maze, Orange Cliffs, and Horseshoe Canyon sections of the park.

- No wood fires are allowed, either in the vehicle campsites or while backpacking.

- Vehicle campers can have charcoal fires, but they must use a fire pan and remove the ashes along with other garbage. Pans can be purchased at the Hans Flat Ranger Station.

- Anybody using the vehicle campsites in the Maze District or Orange Cliffs Unit of Glen Canyon NRA must have and use a portable toilet (not an ammo can or plastic bag) and remove human waste along with all other garbage. Portable toilets can be purchased at the Hans Flat Ranger Station.

- Backpackers can bury their human waste, but they must carry out their toilet paper.

- Backpacking camping is at large but there are limits set for each backcountry zone. You don't need to get your backpacking permit until you get to Hans Flat, but you'll be wise to call in advance for a reservation. Don't make the effort to get there and then find out that you can't go backpacking because your chosen zone is full.

- Backpacking group size limit is 5 people.

- Vehicle permits have a limit of 9 people and 3 vehicles, with the exception of Flint Seep, where up to 16 people can camp.

- In Horseshoe Canyon, groups larger than 20 people must be accompanied by a ranger. To arrange for a guided tour, call the Hans Flat Ranger Station at (801) 259-6513.

- Pets are not allowed (even in your vehicle) in Canyonlands National Park, including Horseshoe Canyon.

- Off-trail hiking in the Doll House area is prohibited.

- ATVs are not allowed in Canyonlands National Park and Glen Canyon National Recreation Area.

WHAT KIND OF VEHICLE TO BRING TO THE MAZE

Unless you wish to hike great distances, you can't fully experience the Maze without a high-clearance four-wheel-drive vehicle.

You can see small parts of the Maze District with a high-clearance, two-wheel-drive vehicle, but to see the best parts, you'll have to park it and hike long distances. A high-clearance four-wheel-drive is absolutely necessary to negotiate the difficult jeep trails in many sections of the Maze District. A long wheel base is problematic in a few spots, but you can usually get through them by backing up to make a tight corner.

The roads in the Maze can deteriorate rapidly when it rains and become treacherous regardless of what kind of vehicle you have. At the same time, fortunately, they dry out relatively fast. If you get caught in a big rain, it's best to wait a few hours for the roads to dry.

CALL IN ADVANCE

The staff at the Hans Flat Ranger Station is trained to help you and eager to answer your questions on the phone. That's much better for both you and the NPS because it's much more difficult to deal with lack of preparation once you're already there. Call in advance at (801) 259-2652. If for some reason, you can't get through on the Hans Flat phone system, call the park headquarters at (801) 259-7164. For reservations for vehicle campsites in the Maze, call the park reservation office at (801) 259-4351. (See page 2 for more on the park's reservation system.)

MOUNTAIN BIKING THE MAZE

Mountain biking is allowed on all designated roads (but not on trails or off-road) in the Maze District. Later in this chapter, detailed descriptions for each road include conditions for mountain biking. If you opt for a mountain biking adventure in the Maze, carefully plan your trip. The NPS offers the following suggestions:

- Take a first-aid kit.
- Check your bike carefully before leaving, and take a bike repair kit.
- Take at least 1 gallon of water per day per biker.
- Take a lock to secure your bike if you plan to leave it to hike, instead of riding or pushing your bike off the road to hide it.
- To avoid the intense heat of summer, try the spring and fall " shoulder seasons." Be prepared for coolish and unsettled weather.
- Wear helmet and gloves.
- If you want solitude, avoid busy weekends and holidays.

RECOMMENDED MOUNTAIN BIKE ROUTES

You can take the following trips suggested by the NPS or you can, of course, map out your own trip. In any case, be sure to stay on official roads. Mountain bikers can stay overnight at designated vehicle campsites which are described as part of the road descriptions later in this chapter, but bikers are required to have a portable toilet, so a support vehicle is necessary.

- *East Rim of Horseshoe Canyon.* Overnight trip, 44 miles round-trip from Hans Flat Ranger Station.
- *Panorama Point and Cleopatra's Chair.* Day or overnight trip, 20 miles round-trip from Hans Flat Ranger Station.
- *Lands End and Big Ridge.* Day or overnight trip, 32 miles round-trip from Hans Flat Ranger Station.
- *Maze Overlook.* Overnight or multi-night trip, 40 miles round-trip from the top of Flint Trail or 68 miles round-trip from Hans Flat Ranger Station.
- *Land of Standing Rock/Doll House.* Multi-night trip, 50 miles round-trip from the top of Flint Trail or 78 miles round-trip from Hans Flat Ranger Station.

GETTING THERE CAN BE HALF THE FUN

I'm not sure what the opinions of locals have to do with any-thing, but when I was on my way to the Maze, I started thinking that I had to drive lots of miles on backcountry roads and I might run short on gas. So I stopped in Green River to top off the tank.

Somewhat foolishly, it seems, I pointed at the map and asked the gas station attendant if I could find a gas station anywhere down there. "Gas station? You'll be lucky if you find a building down there," he responded, rolling his eyes at his co-worker. He wasn't joking.

Undaunted, I later asked a waitress for directions to Hans Flat. She gave them to me, but said "there's nothing but desert out there, and if you go out there you should have your will in order."

I was anxious to start hiking early the next morning, so I de-cided to drive down that night. It was a good two-wheel-drive road all the way, but it was really lonely. For nearly 30 miles, not even a light, not a sign, not another vehicle, nothing. I thought I saw a light once, but that was Venus. Shortly thereafter, a jack-rabbit jumped out and almost gave me a heart attack.

Finally, I saw a sign showing the way to Horseshoe Canyon, and then, 5 miles later, another sign and a junction with the left fork leading to Hans Flat Ranger Station. But there were still no lights or buildings until I reached the ranger station. That's nearly 70 miles of remoteness, quite the culture shock for people used to driving on freeways.

So if you go the Maze, don't worry about getting caught in a traffic jam or for that matter, seeing any signs of civilization.

55 THE GREAT GALLERY

Type of trail:	Out-and-back.
Type of trip:	Day hike (closed to overnight camping).
Total distance:	6.5 miles (round-trip).
Time required:	4-6 hours.
Maps:	Trails Illustrated Maze District/Northeast Glen Canyon and USGS Sugarloaf Butte.
Difficulty:	Moderate.
Starting point:	West rim trailhead.

Finding the trailhead: There are two ways to get to Horseshoe Canyon. You can take the hike down from the west rim (as described here) or you can drive into the canyon from the east (as described on page 186). To get to the west rim trailhead, go 5 miles north of the junction between the Hanksville and Green River access roads to the Maze, and watch for a small sign on the east side of the road that says "Horseshoe Canyon Foot Trail 2 miles." From here, drive 2 miles on a two-wheel-drive road to the trailhead.

The hike: Although officially a "detached unit" of Canyonlands National Park, the Horseshoe Canyon area could be better described as a little hidden jewel lost in the desert. It's definitely worth the time it takes to get there. If you already plan on a few days in the Maze, you won't be disappointed if you spend a half-day of your vacation at Horseshoe Canyon. If you're going to the Maze from Green River, Horseshoe Canyon is a convenient stop.

The Great Gallery is one of four major rock art sites in Horseshoe Canyon, but the fabulous rock art is only part of the attraction. Horseshoe Canyon would be well worth the stop without it. It's a great day hike in a secluded canyon with majestic cottonwoods shading the sheer sandstone cliffs.

Horseshoe Canyon has one other unusual trait. It's one of the few places in the Canyonlands with a fairly reliable water supply that is devoid of the evil tamarisk. NPS volunteers removed all of the "tammies" a few years back, and now, cottonwoods and other native vegetation are reclaiming the canyon.

Rangers lead a hike into the canyon at 9 a.m. on Saturdays during the summer, but this is always subject to change, so call the Hans Flat Ranger Station at (801) 259-2652 to verify the schedule. If you have a large group but can't fit into the regular schedule, you may be able to arrange a special ranger-led tour. If you have a group of 20 or more people, you are required to have a ranger along.

Viewing the Great Gallery.

You don't have to go with the ranger, but it's the best way to get a more complete story and history of Horseshoe Canyon. The ranger stops at each of the four rock art sites to explain the history and prehistory, and also comments on the natural history of the hidden canyon along the way. If you want to get good photographs of the rock art panels at the Great Gallery, early afternoon light is usually best.

The hike starts out on and follows an old road from the west rim to the canyon floor. Since it's a road, the grade is not too steep. Nonetheless, it drops 750 feet in elevation in about 1.5 miles, which can get the heart rate up on the way back. The road is mostly slickrock at the upper end and turns to loose sand as you approach the canyon floor. This adds to the difficulty of climbing back out. Be sure to bring water.

On the way down you can see the remains of historic ranching operations (fences, pipes, water troughs, etc.). You can also see the austere four-wheel-drive road that drops into the canyon from the east rim. When you reach the canyon floor, the trail turns right and follows the canyon bottom for 1.75 miles to the Great Gallery.

A ranger often stays much of the day at the Great Gallery to answer questions. On the way into the Great Gallery, the first two rock art panels have interpretive displays. Watch for short side trails, so you don't miss any of them, but if you do, you can catch them on the way back.

Rock art is extremely fragile and extremely precious, so don't touch any of the figures or disturb any artifacts found in the canyon. These are irreplaceable treasures. Don't cross over the chain barriers placed around the rock art by the NPS.

THE GREAT GALLERY

© National Geographic/Trails Illustrated

Holy Ghost and Attendants at the Great Gallery in Horseshoe Canyon.

The rock art in Horseshoe Canyon is considered an example of the "Barrier Canyon" style, which dates back to the late Archaic period from 2,000 to 1,000 B.C. Later, the ancestral Puebloan cultures left their marks in the canyon, but apparently stayed only briefly. These early cultures were followed by modern cultures—cattle and sheep ranchers, oil prospectors, miners, and now, park visitors. Throughout all this use, however, the special character of the canyon has been wonderfully preserved. All visitors have the responsibility to do their part to keep it that way.

The Great Gallery is the last of four interpretive stops made by the ranger. It's a sprawling rock art panel with large, intricate figures, both pictographs (painted figures) and petroglyphs (figures etched in the stone with a sharp object). When you reach the Great Gallery, stop for lunch, rest awhile, and marvel at a few things. For example, even though the pictographs have faded slightly through the centuries, how did the early cultures come up with a "paint" that lasted three thousand years? What do the paintings really mean? What type of religious ceremonies might have occurred here? The ranger might toss out a few theories, and the NPS keeps some interpretive information at the Great Gallery, but nobody really knows what went on at the Great Gallery thirty centuries ago.

Type of trail:	Out-and-back.
Type of trip:	Long day hike or overnighter.
Total distance:	14 miles.
Time required:	7-10 hours.
Maps:	Trails Illustrated Maze District/Northeast Glen Canyon and USGS Gordon Flats and Elaterite Basin.
Difficulty:	Difficult.
Starting point:	North Point Trailhead.

Finding the trailhead: To get to the North Trail Trailhead, drive 2.5 miles from Hans Flat and turn right (north) at the junction with the Panorama Point Road. Go another 0.9 mile and park on the left across from the trailhead sign. You can also park at the Panorama Point Junction and hike down the road to the trailhead.

The hike: For hikers who don't have a four-wheel-drive vehicle or don't want to drive the Maze roads, the North Trail provides access to the Maze.

THE NORTH TRAIL

© National Geographic/Trails Illustrated

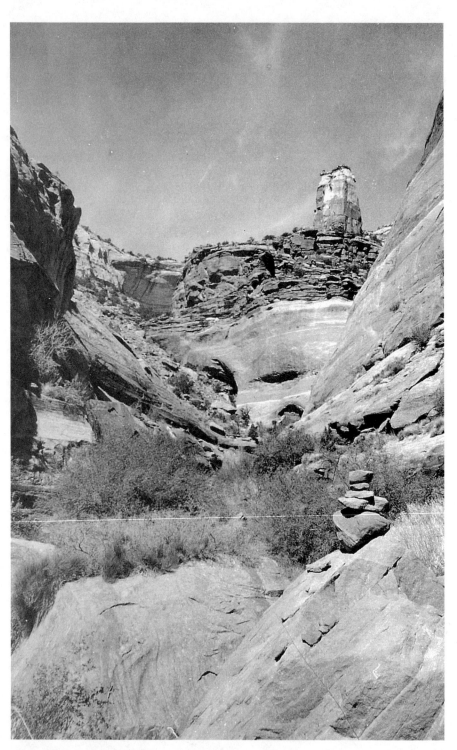

One short section of the North Trail is fairly rugged.

Lining packs down Maze Overlook Trail.

It's for serious backpackers, though, since it's 15 miles one-way to the Maze Overlook—the first 7 miles on designated trail, and the rest of it on primitive roads. When you get to the Maze Overlook Trailhead, it's a short but tough mile-long drop into the Maze where you can camp at-large per park regulations.

The North Trail starts out flat and well defined through the junipers and pinyon pines on North Point Mesa. After about a mile, the trail drops into North Trail Canyon. The first part of the descent follows well-marked switchbacks. Then, near the bottom, there's a half-mile stretch of nearly trailless route-finding. There's no chance of getting off the trail, however, since it follows the narrow canyon.

After this one difficult stretch, the trail comes back, but stays rocky and rough as it follows the dry wash of North Trail Canyon for 2 miles. Then, the valley opens up, and the trail gets easy and well defined on packed dirt, similar to the first mile up on the North Point Mesa. It stays that way over the last 3 miles to the junction with the Millard Canyon Road.

Near the end, you cross over a small ridge into the West Fork of Big Water Canyon just before the trail-road junction. You're now in Elaterite Basin. Massive Elaterite Butte dominates the horizon to the southeast, and to the north, you can see equally massive Ekker Butte and Panorama Point.

If you're continuing on to the Maze Overlook, take a right (south) when you reach the road. If you'll be returning this way later, note the surroundings. There's no trailhead sign here.

If you plan to stay overnight and then return to the trailhead the next day, or if you started late and need a campsite for your first night on your way to the Maze Overlook, you can find many excellent choices along the easternmost 3 miles of the trail.

Type of trail:	Out-and-back.
Type of trip:	Day hike or base camp for overnighter.
Total distance:	3 miles.
Time required:	1-2 hours.
Maps:	Trails Illustrated Maze District/Northeast Glen Canyon and USGS Gordon Flats and Clearwater Canyon.
Difficulty:	Moderate.
Starting point:	Trailhead at end of Happy Canyon spur road.

Finding the trailhead: From Hans Flat Ranger Station, drive 2.5 miles to the Panorama Point Junction and take a right (south) onto the Gordon Flats Road. After 12.1 miles, pass by the left turn to the Flint Trail and keep going straight for another 1.3 miles until you see the right-hand turn (west) to Happy Canyon Camp. Turn here and go 0.4 mile to the camp on your left and another 0.1 mile to the end of the road, a parking area, and the trailhead.

The hike: This trail is actually an abandoned jeep road. That means a fairly easy grade, but the lack of maintenance on the road makes going

HAPPY CANYON, GOLDEN STAIRS

© National Geographic/Trails Illustrated

tougher than it normally would be. The trail doesn't receive much use, so it doesn't get high priority on the maintenance schedule. The plus side of this, of course, is that it's usually devoid of people, so you can have a nice part of the Canyonlands all to yourself.

After 1.5 miles, the trail ends as it reaches the floor of Happy Canyon. From here, you can strike off in any direction to explore or set up your backpack camp. On the way down the trail, you get a sweeping view of the broad, flat Happy Canyon. You might want to take a few minutes on the way down to spot a few places you might want to explore when you reach the end of the trail.

This is also a great choice for people who have only a two-wheel-drive vehicle. The road to the trailhead can be covered without a four-wheel-drive vehicle, but there are a few rocky sections where you need to go very slowly and use great care. The NPS considers this an "overflow area" and recommends it when the Maze campsites fill up.

58 THE GOLDEN STAIRS

See Map on Facing Page

Type of trail:	Out-and-back.
Type of trip:	Day hike.
Total distance:	4 miles.
Time required:	3-4 hours.
Maps:	Trails Illustrated Maze District/Northeast Glen Canyon and USGS Elaterite Basin.
Difficulty:	Moderate.
Starting point:	Golden Stairs Camp.

Finding the trailhead: From Hans Flat Ranger Station, drive 2.5 miles to the Panorama Point Junction and take a right (south) onto the Gordon Flats Road. After 12.1 miles, turn left (east) and head down the Flint Trail switchbacks for 2.8 miles to the Maze Overlook Road where you take a left (north). About 2.6 miles down this road, watch for a sign indicating a right turn (east) to the Golden Stairs Camp. In 2 miles, this

spur road deadends at the Golden Stairs Camp, a parking area, and the trailhead. The trailhead is on the east side of the camp, not at the parking area where you might expect to find it. The trailhead does not have a sign, so watch for a "no bicycles" sign and a string of cairns heading off to the east.

The hike: If you're staying at the Golden Stairs Camp, you'll want to take a delightful evening or early morning walk down the Golden Stairs. For those who don't have the high-clearance four-wheel-drive vehicle necessary to make it over the Teapot Rock section of the Doll House Road, this trail also can be used as a way to backpack into Ernie's Country.

From the trail, you get an expansive view of much of the Maze district, including the sprawling Ernie's Country, the Fins, and even a distant glimpse of the Land of Standing Rocks. You can also see the road to the Doll House as it passes through the rugged Teapot Rock Country.

For the first half-mile, the trail passes through juniper and pinyon pine on a mesa. Shortly after leaving the trailhead, you pass over China Neck, a narrow "bridge" between two sections of the mesa with steep cliffs on both sides. If you have children with you, watch them carefully.

Soon after crossing the narrow section, the trail drops off the mesa and takes a big curve to the right, gradually descending. The grade is fairly mild as the trail traverses along the face of the cliff until the 1.5-mile mark where it drops sharply down to the road. During this short steep section, you go through a series of gold-colored sandstone ledges commonly referred to as the Golden Stairs. It's difficult to see them while hiking down, but on the way back, they're much more visible. Also, on the way back, you get a great view to the north of The Mother and Child.

Although it's difficult to imagine when you're hiking this trail, it actually follows a historic route used by ranchers to get their stock up to the mesa to graze. The trail goes over slickrock or loose rock most of the way. It isn't suited for fast hiking, but it's well-marked and easy to follow.

At the east end of the trail where it meets the road, there is no sign. Instead, a huge cairn marks the trailhead.

59   MAZE OVERLOOK

Type of trail:	Out-and-back.
Type of trip:	Day hike or first leg of multi-day trip.
Total distance:	3 miles (round-trip) not counting any off-trail hiking.
Time required:	3-4 hours.
Maps:	Trails Illustrated Maze District/Northeast Glen Canyon and USGS Elaterite Basin and Spanish Bottom.
Difficulty:	Difficult.
Starting point:	Maze Overlook Trailhead and parking area.

Finding the trailhead: From Hans Flat Ranger Station, take a right at the Panorama Point Road Junction at the 2.5-mile mark. At the 12.1-mile mark, turn left (east) and head down the Flint Trail. At the 14.4-mile mark, you hit the junction with the Maze Overlook Road. Take a left and go an-

© National Geographic/Trails Illustrated

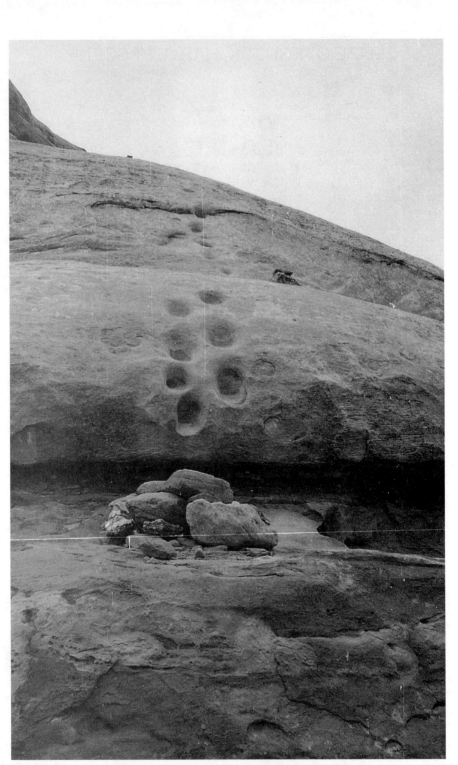

Slickrock "steps" help hikers get down the Maze Overlook Trail.

other 8.1 miles to the junction with the Millard Canyon Road. Take a right here, and go 5 miles to the Maze Overlook.

The hike: Before you head down the trail, take a few minutes to survey the landscape. They call this place the Maze Overlook because you get a great overview of the well-named Maze. The magnificent Chocolate Drops highlight the southern horizon, and you can see Standing Rock, Chimney Rock, Lizard Rock, and many other famous landmarks of the Maze District from here.

The Maze Overlook Trail is not for beginners or hikers afraid of heights. It's short, only about a mile, but it drops 600 feet in elevation and gets fairly steep and exposed in places, requiring you to use your hands for safety.

Over the first part of the trail, try not to get too absorbed by the scenery and miss the next cairn. The trail meanders back and forth, using ledges as a safe route to the canyon bottom. Then, the trail strikes off across the slickrock. It goes through two tight joints which might be too narrow for a overstuffed backpack, and in two or three places, you might want to use a rope to lower your backpack to be safe. Slickrock steps, chipped out of solid rock, help you get down the steepest parts of the trail.

Even though the trail seems rough, actually, it's expertly constructed to get down a difficult route to the floor of the Maze. With a little care, the Maze Overlook Trail can be perfectly safe.

Once you get to the bottom, you'll see a major seep where, if necessary, you can get water. However, be sure to purify it before drinking. From this point, you can head off in several directions, following canyons through the Maze.

60 HARVEST SCENE

See Map on Page 177

Type of trail:	Loop.
Type of trip:	Long day hike or overnighter.
Total distance:	12 miles.
Time required:	7-10 hours.
Maps:	Trails Illustrated Maze District/Northeast Glen Canyon and USGS Spanish Bottom.
Difficulty:	Difficult.
Starting point:	Chimney Rock Trailhead.

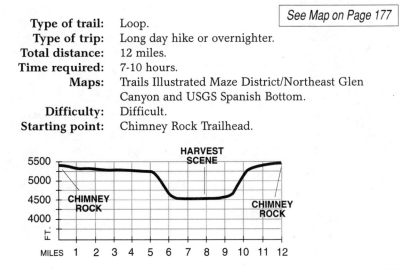

Finding the trailhead: From Hans Flat Ranger Station, drive 2.5 miles to the Panorama Point Junction and take a right (south) onto the Gordon Flats Road. After 12.1 miles, turn left (east) and head down the Flint Trail switchbacks for 2.8 miles to the Maze Overlook Road where you take a right (south). Follow this road through Waterhole Flat for 3.5 miles to a four-way junction with the Doll House Road. Turn left (northeast) and head for the Doll House and Land of Standing Rocks. The map might show a cut-off trail where it looks like you can save some time, but this is deceptively incorrect. You actually can make faster time on the longer route because of the excellent roads in this section. Once on the Doll House Road, stay on it for 17.1 miles to the Chimney Rock Camp. At the east end of the camp, you'll find a parking area and a major trailhead. The trails aren't signed, but watch for strings of cairns heading off on each side of Chimney Rock which mark the two trails you want for the Harvest Scene Loop.

The hike: This trail is not only a rare loop (most Maze trails are out-and-back), but it's also the longest designated trail in the Maze. If you're in the vicinity with an extra day at your disposal, you will be rewarded by spending that time on this long day hike. You can also backpack and camp at-large in the area, which has several great campsites.

The trail goes to one of the most famous rock art sites in the world, Harvest Scene. Plus, it passes through two beautiful canyons indicative to hiking terrain that has made the Maze so popular. The difference is that you're on designated routes instead of off-trail canyon routes.

Even though the routes are designated and marked by cairns, this hike is

Standing water in an unnamed canyon just before reaching the Harvest Scene.

not for total beginners. It requires some steep climbs and experience in following routes marked only (and sometime sparsely) with cairns. Most of the trail goes over slickrock or follows canyon wash, and there are several side canyons quite capable of confusing the hiker. Cairns mark the trail, but backpackers sometimes set up unofficial cairns to mark the location of their camp and cairns sometimes fall down, so you must be able to find the correct way on your own. Keep your topo map in hand all the way, constantly noting your location.

This trail description follows the counterclockwise route, not because it's easier, but because it's slightly less confusing at one critical spot where you turn out of one canyon into another. To take the counterclockwise route, start on the trail just east of Chimney Rock. Be careful not to start on a trail on the far east end of the parking area. This is an off-trail route up Shot and Water Canyons.

The first section of trail stays on top of a slickrock ridge between two unnamed canyons. In some sections the cairns are sparse, so stay alert. To your right, you can see into precipitous Jasper Canyon, which is closed to all entry to preserve a unique biological resource.

At the 3.5-mile mark, the trail takes a sharp left and makes a steep but safe descent into the dry wash of an unnamed canyon. This is the most confusing stretch of the hike, so keep the topo map out and note your progress carefully. There are at least three side canyons that could get you lost.

After a mile walk in this canyon, you reach a major junction of canyons. It's not an exaggeration to say that canyons head off in every direction. You need to take the sharp left into an unnamed canyon and head for the Harvest Scene (named on most maps). If there's any doubt in your mind, backtrack or take the extra time to make sure you're headed in the right direction.

Any doubts you have will be erased after about a half-mile when you see the spectacular Harvest Scene rock art panel on your right. (Just before you get to Harvest Scene, you get a good view of the massive Chocolate Drops formation on the canyon rim near the Maze Overlook Camps.)

Like other rock art panels, the Harvest Scene is an extremely precious treasure, so don't touch or damage the rock art in any way. It has lasted three thousand years, and if all park visitors treat it with exceptional care, it might last another three thousand years.

After a long break at Harvest Scene continue south down the unnamed Maze canyon, a side canyon to sprawling Horse Canyon. Again, keep the topo map out to make sure you don't accidentally get in the wrong canyon.

Both canyons you follow on this hike have intermittent and unreliable water sources. On many spring hikes, you can see little gem-like pools with their biotic communities of snails, worms, and water striders.

After a pleasant 3-mile walk up Petroglyph Fork, you climb up to the canyon rim. This is a fairly steep, but short, climb. From this point, it's an easy mile or so on slickrock back to Chimney Rock.

Type of trail:	Out-and-back.
Type of trip:	Long day trip or overnighter.
Total distance:	9 miles.
Time required:	5-8 hours.
Maps:	Trails Illustrated Maze District/Northeast Glen Canyon and USGS Spanish Bottom.
Difficulty:	Moderate.
Starting point:	Trailhead just before the Doll House Camps.

Finding the trailhead: From Hans Flat Ranger Station, drive 2.5 miles to the Panorama Point Junction and take a right (south) onto the Gordon Flats Road. After 12.1 miles, turn left (east) and head down the Flint Trail switchbacks for 2.8 miles to the Big Water Canyon Road where you take a right (south). Follow this road along an exposed ledge and down a steep dugway for 3.5 miles to a four-way junction with the Doll House Road. Turn left (northeast) and head for the Doll House and Land of Standing Rocks. The map might show a cut off trail that looks like it can save some

COLORADO/GREEN RIVER OVERLOOK, SPANISH BOTTOM, THE GRANARY

© National Geographic/Trails Illustrated

time, but this is deceptively incorrect. You actually can make faster time on the longer route because of the excellent roads in this section. Once on the Doll House Road, stay on it for 20.8 miles to the Doll House Camps. When you get to the Doll House area, the road forks with Doll House 3 Camp on the right and Doll House 1 and Doll House 2 on the left. Take a left, and you'll find the trailhead on your left about 100 feet before you turn again to Doll House 1 Camp.

The hike: This is the longest, and perhaps most spectacular, of the three designated hikes in the Doll House area. It traverses all types of terrain—canyon wash, open parks, narrow joints, slickrock. It even goes by massive Beehive Arch on its way to lofty overlooks where you can see the mighty Colorado River absorbing the equally mighty Green River and heading south to Cataract Canyon.

If you only have time for one day hike during your stay in the Doll House, this would be a great choice. If you're in the mood to backpack, you can find many excellent at-large campsites along this route.

The first mile or so of the trail wanders its way through the spires of the Doll House, going right by Beehive Arch. If you're only interested in a short, flat day hike, you can turn around after investigating the massive arch.

After you leave the Doll House area, the trail drops into the dry wash of an unnamed canyon, which forks once with the trail going right. Watch for cairns here; if you aren't paying attention, you could go straight and get off the trail. After about 3 miles, you climb out of the dry wash and the trail goes through several open parks with sandstone spires on the horizon.

Next, you pass through two narrow canyons between the sandstone formations before reaching the beginning of a small loop. The little loop trail at the end of this hike might not be marked with a sign, and it can be confusing. Get your map out and check it carefully. Along the loop you can strike off to the southeast or northeast along slickrock ledges to get magnificent views of the Colorado and Green rivers.

On the way back, don't miss the spot where the trail leaves the dry wash and goes off to the left. It would be relatively easy to keep going straight and be temporarily lost.

See Map on Page 182

Type of trail:	Out-and-back.
Type of trip:	Day hike.
Total distance:	3 miles.
Time required:	2-4 hours.
Maps:	Trails Illustrated Maze District/Northeast Glen Canyon and USGS Spanish Bottom.
Difficulty:	Moderate.
Starting point:	Trailhead just before turn to Doll House 1 Camp.

Finding the trailhead: When you get to the Doll House area, the road forks with the right fork going to the Doll House 3 Camp and the left fork going to Doll House 1 and Doll House 2. Take a left, and you'll find the trailhead about 50 feet after the trailhead going to the Confluence Overlook and 50 feet before you turn again to Doll House 1 Camp.

The hike: The Spanish Bottom trail drops steeply from the trailhead all the way down to the Colorado River, hitting the river just after the Colorado has absorbed the Green River.

Even though the trail drops about 1,100 feet in about a mile, it's still the easiest way to get to the Colorado River from the Doll House area. The well-constructed trail with frequent switchbacks partly mitigates the steepness. The trail is well-defined and marked the entire way.

The first fourth-mile of the trail is nice and flat as it curves between the stunning sandstone towers of the Doll House. Then, shortly after you take a left at the junction with the Granary Trail, the Spanish Bottom Trail starts descending.

For most of the way down, you can see the large and extremely flat Spanish Bottom and the Colorado River flowing by it. You might see some campers, too, since this is a popular campsite for people floating the river. They like to camp here to gather their courage for the thunderous Cataract Canyon just around the bend in the river.

When you get to the bottom, take a break and relax for a while—and, of course, amass your strength for a steep climb up to the Doll House. The sharp incline makes this a great trail to hike in the coolish temperatures of the early morning or early evening.

63   THE GRANARY

See Map on Page 182

Type of trail:	Partial loop.
Type of trip:	Day hike.
Total distance:	2 miles.
Time required:	1-2 hours.
Maps:	Trails Illustrated Maze District/Northeast Glen Canyon and USGS Spanish Bottom.
Difficulty:	Easy.
Starting point:	Trailhead just before turn to Doll House 1 Camp.

Finding the trailhead: Follow the same directions used for the Spanish Bottom hike.

The hike: The first part of the hike (which follows the same route as the Spanish Bottom Trail) is actually part of a small loop. Start out on the same trail described above for Spanish Bottom. After less than a half-mile of flat, easy hiking through the Doll House towers, you reach a junction. Take a right (west) here and head to the Granary instead dropping off the edge of the plateau to Spanish Bottom.

After another quarter mile of easy walking, you reach yet another junction, with the Granary trail going to the left. The right fork takes you back to the trailhead, and you'll take it after you visit the Granary and see Surprise Valley.

Just before you reach the Granary, you'll see an overlook on your left only a few feet off the trail. From here you get a spectacular vista of Surprise Valley, a classic graben and a gorgeous one at that. About another 100 yards up the trail is the Granary, a typical storage place used by the ancestral Puebloan cultures to hide away grain for the lean winter months.

On the way back, be sure to take the left fork at the first junction. This follows a well-laid out route through the Doll House, including a long stretch through joints in the sandstone formations. The entire trail is well defined, mostly packed dirt and easy to follow.

BACKCOUNTRY ROADS

The backcountry roads of the Maze should probably be viewed as trails that vehicles and mountain bikes use instead of as roads. The conditions are primitive, so you must be prepared—both mentally—and with a vehicle in excellent condition.

15 HORSESHOE CANYON

Starting point:	Hans Flat Ranger Station.
Total distance:	From Hans Flat, 22 miles (one way) to the bottom of Horseshoe Canyon
Key points:	10.0 Turnoff to High Spur Camp.
	12.0 Leave Glen Canyon NRA.
	12.6 Turnoff to Deadman's Trail.
	20.0 Rim of Horseshoe Canyon.
	22.0 Bottom of Horseshoe Canyon.
Time required:	To High Spur Camp, 1 hour; to canyon rim, 2 hours; to the bottom of canyon, 2.5 hours.
Maps:	Trails Illustrated Maze District/Northeast Glen Canyon and USGS Head Spur and Sugarloaf Butte.
Permits:	Permit required for vehicle camping at the High Spur campsite. Camping is not permitted in Horseshoe Canyon.
Minimum vehicle requirements:	First 5 miles, low-clearance two-wheel-drive; to rim of canyon, high-clearance four-wheel-drive; to the bottom of canyon, high-clearance four-wheel-drive; on Deadman's Trail, high-clearance four-wheel-drive; on the side road to High Spur Camp, high-clearance four-wheel-drive.
Difficulty:	Easy to canyon rim, extremely difficult into canyon.
Road conditions:	Excellent the first 5 miles, then conditions worsen slightly. It's packed dirt and loose sand with a few short rocky sections all the way to rim of Horseshoe Canyon. The road down into the canyon is rocky, steep, narrow, and technical four-wheeling. Most people stop at the rim of canyon and walk the road into canyon. Grazing is allowed in Glen Canyon NRA, so watch for cattle on the road.
Suitability for mountain biking:	Flat except for the drop into the canyon, easy going in most places with a few stretches of loose sand in first 10 miles and near the canyon rim. Side roads to High Spur Camp and up Deadman's Trail are also excellent for mountain biking.

Vehicle camps:	High Spur Camp on east side of road 10 miles north of Hans Flat, 1 mile off main road and in the shadow of a huge sandstone formation, which rises abruptly out of the mesa. Get a great view of Cleopatra's Chair which really looks like a chair from here. Grazing is allowed in Glen Canyon NRA, so you could have a cow in camp.
Special attractions:	Spectacular Horseshoe Canyon.
Special precautions:	Watch for cattle on the road. If you decide to drive into Horseshoe Canyon, go slowly and carefully.

16 NORTH POINT

Starting point:	Hans Flat Ranger Station.
Total distance:	From Gordon Flats Road, 7 miles (one way) to where road splits to Cleopatra's Chair and Panorama Point.
Time required:	1 hour (one way).
Maps:	Trails Illustrated Maze District/Northeast Glen Canyon and USGS Elaterite Basin and Cleopatra's Chair.
Permits:	Vehicle camping or at-large backpacking permit required. Day use allowed with no permit.
Minimum vehicle requirements:	High-clearance four-wheel-drive.
Difficulty:	Moderate.
Road conditions:	Mostly through juniper and pinyon pines on the mesa. Several long, very steep, rocky sections intermingled with smooth sections of packed dirt. There is some loose sand with one mile-long smooth section through a big open park. Good scenery most of the way.
Suitability for mountain biking:	Mostly excellent conditions—flat terrain, packed dirt with a few rocky sections and some loose sand.

17 PANORAMA POINT

Starting point:	End of North Point Road.
Total distance:	From end of North Point Road, 2 miles (one way) to Panorama Point overlook and camp.
Time required:	20-30 minutes (one way).
Maps:	Trails Illustrated Maze District/Northeast Glen Canyon and USGS Cleopatra's Chair.
Permits:	Vehicle camping or at-large backpacking permit required. Day use allowed with no permit.

The truly panoramic view from Panorama Point.

Minimum vehicle requirements:	High-clearance four-wheel-drive.
Difficulty:	Moderate.
Road conditions:	Packed dirt with frequent rocky sections and ledges and a long stretch of solid slickrock near the end of the road. Truly spectacular scenery from Panorama Point.
Suitability for mountain biking:	Excellent conditions.
Hiking:	From camp, you can hike off-trail north along the rim of the mesa, but be careful not to get too close to the edge of the steep cliff.
Vehicle camps:	Panorama Point is probably the most scenic campsite in the Maze—or anywhere else! There's a great vista down into Elaterite Basin with the Maze in the distance to the east and Ekker Butte to the north and Elaterite Butte to the south. The camp is right at the end of the road in junipers and pinyon pines and just a few feet from the edge of the cliff, so if you have children, watch them carefully. Panorama Point may be closed to camping in the spring due to nesting peregrine falcons, so be sure to check with a ranger before making your final plans.
Special attractions:	World-famous view from end of road.
Special precautions:	Extremely steep cliff at end of road and near camp. Very exposed and windy.

Total distance:	From end of North Point Road, 3 miles (one way) to end of road and Cleopatra's Chair Camp.
Time required:	20-30 minutes (one way).
Maps:	Trails Illustrated Maze District/Northeast Glen Canyon and USGS Cleopatra's Chair.
Permits:	Vehicle camping or at-large backpacking permit required. Day use allowed with no permit.
Minimum vehicle requirements:	High-clearance four-wheel-drive.
Road conditions:	Mostly packed dirt with a few short rocky sections.
Suitability for mountain biking:	Excellent conditions.
Hiking:	From camp, you can take a short (4 miles round-trip) off-trail hike out to the north end of North Point Mesa. It's a delightful hike, but be sure to have your topo map along.
Vehicle camps:	Cleopatra's Chair Camp is at the end of the road in the south shadow of massive Cleopatra's Chair (which really doesn't look like a chair from this viewpoint) and about 100 feet from a great overlook into sprawling Millard Canyon.
Special precautions:	Be extra cautious around the steep cliff at end of road and near camp.

Camping below massive Cleopatra's Chair.

19 GORDON FLATS

Total distance: From Hans Flat Ranger Station, 12.1 miles (one way) to where the road forks with left-hand fork going down the Flint Trail and the right-hand fork going to the Big Ridge.

Key points:
2.2 French's Cabin.
2.4 French's Spring.
2.5 Panorama Point Road.
9.1 Bagpipe Butte Overlook.
11.1 Flint Seep Camp.
11.9 Flint Trail Overlook.
12.1 Flint Trail/The Big Ridge Junction.

Time required: 1 hour (one way).

Maps: Trails Illustrated Maze District/Northeast Glen Canyon and USGS Gordon Flats.

Permits: Vehicle camping or at-large backpacking permit required. Day use allowed without a permit.

Minimum vehicle requirements: Low-clearance two-wheel-drive.

Road conditions: One of the best roads in the Maze/Orange Cliffs area, mostly packed dirt. It can be driven with almost any vehicle.

Suitability for mountain biking: Excellent conditions.

Vehicle camps: Flint Seep Camp is only about 100 yards west of the Gordon Flats Road nestled in a grove of junipers and pinyon pines. This camp has been established as a group site with a limit of 16 people and 5 vehicles. Call the park reservation office to reserve this campsite.

20 THE BIG RIDGE

Total distance: 8 miles (one way) from Flint Trail junction to Glen Canyon NRA boundary.

Key points (from Flint Trail/Gordon Flats Junction):
0.9 Turn to Happy Canyon.
2.3 The Neck Camp.
7.1 Glen Canyon NRA Boundary.

Time required: 1-2 hours (one way).

Maps: Trails Illustrated Maze District/Northeast Glen Canyon and USGS Gordon Flats and Clearwater Canyon.

Permits: Vehicle camping or at-large backpacking permit required. Day use allowed with no permit.

Minimum vehicle	
requirements:	High-clearance two-wheel-drive
Road conditions:	More rocky than most roads in the area, but not extreme. Mostly flat as it stays on top of the Big Ridge Mesa. Gets worse after the Neck, even rockier and some bad gullies. Goes through juniper and pinyon pines most of the way. About 3 miles past the park boundary (around the old Simplot Landing Strip), the road becomes impassable.
Suitability for	
mountain biking:	Flat, mostly packed dirt, with minimal loose sand with frequent short rocky sections.
Hiking:	From Happy Canyon Camp, you can take a designated trail (actually an abandoned road) down to the bottom of Happy Canyon, where it ends after about 1.5 miles. Once in the valley floor, you can explore in any direction.
Vehicle camps:	The Neck Camp is just off the west side of the road where the mesa narrows into a narrow "neck" like a similar spot in the Island in the Sky. Good scenery from the campsite. To get to Happy Canyon Camp, take the side road heading west off the main road about a mile past the Flint Trail junction and follow it for about 0.4 mile until you see the camp on your left. The road continues on for another 100 yards where it ends at the trailhead for the Happy Canyon Trail and a good view of the Henry Mountains to the south.

21 THE FLINT TRAIL

Total distance:	From Gordon Flats Road, 2.8 miles (one way) to Maze Overlook Road.
Time required:	1 hour (one way).
Maps:	Trails Illustrated Maze District/Northeast Glen Canyon and USGS Clearwater Canyon and Teapot Rock.
Permits:	Vehicle camping or at-large backpacking permit required. Day use allowed without a permit.
Minimum vehicle	
requirements:	High-clearance four-wheel-drive with a short wheel base is best for the tight turns on the switchbacks.
Road conditions:	The first part of the road is a very steep series of switchbacks from The Big Ridge down the Orange Cliffs to another small mesa. When dry, the switchbacks are easily passable with extra attention from the driver. But when wet, the clay gets too slippery to drive. If you get caught in a rainstorm,

wait until the clay dries out before attempting the Flint Trail.

Suitability for mountain biking: Good conditions when dry, but use extreme caution and keep the speed down when going down the switchbacks.

Special precautions: Go slowly on switchbacks and avoid them when wet. Chains are required for all four wheels in winter when snow is on the ground.

---

22 MAZE OVERLOOK

Total distance: From Hans Flat, 27.5 miles (one way) to the Maze Overlook camps. From the junction with Flint Trail, 12.6 miles to the Maze Overlook camps.

Key points (from Flint Trail Junction):
2.6   Golden Stairs turnoff.
10.2   Millard Canyon Junction.
11.8   Canyonlands National Park boundary.
15.4   Maze Overlook camps, trailhead and parking area.

Time required: From Hans Flat Ranger Station, 3-4 hours (one way); from the Flint Trail junction, 2-3 hours (one way).

Maps: Trails Illustrated Maze District/Northeast Glen Canyon and USGS Elaterite Basin and Teapot Rock.

Permits: Vehicle camping or at-large backpacking permit required. Day use allowed with no permit.

Minimum vehicle requirements: High-clearance four-wheel-drive.

Road conditions: Some sections are easy going, but most of the road is rocky (both loose rock and slickrock) with some steep sections and several ledges where clearance is critical. You'll want to get out of your vehicle to carefully check the route. Probably the toughest section is just past the Golden Stairs turnoff, as you drop off the mesa into Big Water Canyon. Great scenery all the way with the Orange Cliffs on the western horizon as you take a big turn around Elaterite Butte.

Suitability for mountain biking: Mostly good conditions with frequent rocky sections and minimal loose sand. Conditions turn to excellent after the junction with the Millard Canyon Road. Spectacular scenery all the way.

Hiking: The Maze Overlook is the springboard to perhaps the greatest hiking in the Canyonlands. Many people backpack into the Maze from the end of this road and stay for several days. Others like to day hike from one of the vehicle camps. You enter the Maze

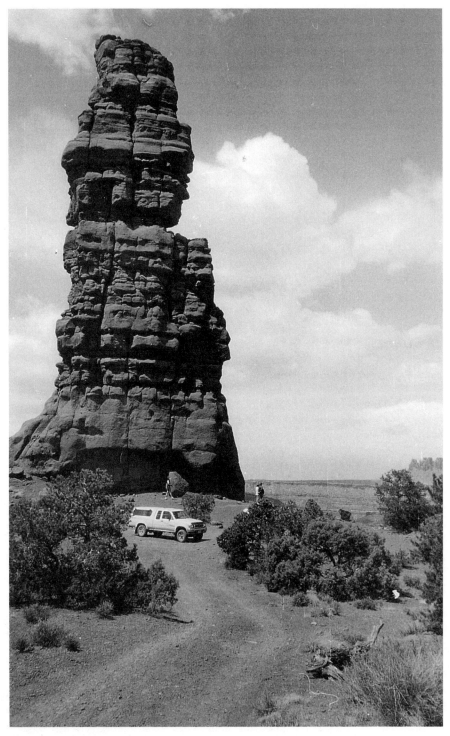

Camping below Standing Rock.

via a short but steep trail starting at the parking area just past the camps. The hiking opportunities from the Maze Overlook, however, aren't for beginners. All trails have steep sections and requires route-finding skills. The area visible from the Maze Overlook Camps is closed to at-large backpacking camps.

Vehicle camps: Both Maze Overlook 1 and Maze Overlook 2 are gorgeous campsites in the shadow of the fabulous Chocolate Drops towers, which are sculpted from Organ Rock shale. You can see it all from these camps: the Maze, Elaterite Butte, Ekker Butte, Panorama Point, the Land of Standing Rock, and even the mighty La Sal Mountains serving as a backdrop to the east. The camps are quite exposed, however, so they can be unpleasant on a windy day. The camps also are extremely popular, so get your reservation in early.

Special attractions: Outstanding scenery along the road and from Maze Overlook camps.

---

23 GOLDEN STAIRS

Total distance: From Maze Overlook Road, 1 mile (one way) to Golden Stairs Camp and parking area.

Time required: 20-30 minutes (one way).

Maps: Trails Illustrated Maze District/Northeast Glen Canyon and USGS Elaterite Basin.

Permits: Vehicle camping or at-large backpacking permit required. Day use allowed with no permit.

Minimum vehicle requirements: High-clearance four-wheel-drive.

Road conditions: Mostly rocky with ledges.

Suitability for mountain biking: Slightly rough mountain biking on this short side road from the Maze Overlook Road to Golden Stairs Camp.

Hiking: From camp, you can take the Golden Stairs trail over China Neck and down to the Doll House Road or hike north off-trail along the edge of the mesa. If you want to explore the mesa, take the Golden Stairs Trail for about a half-mile over China Neck. Shortly thereafter, where the trail takes a sharp right, you can climb to the mesa to the north.

Vehicle camps: Golden Stairs Camp sits up high on a 6,000-foot mesa crowned with junipers and pinyon pines. The view right from camp is not great, but a short walk gives you superb vistas in several directions.

194

24 MILLARD CANYON

Total distance: From Hans Flat Ranger Station, 33.4 miles (one way) to the Green River.

Key points (from the turnoff to the Maze Overlook):
- 0.3   North Trail Trailhead.
- 2.0   Canyonlands National Park boundary (no sign).
- 9.2   Ekker Butte Camp.
- 23.0   Millard Canyon Camp.

Time required: From Hans Flat Ranger Station, 4-5 hours (one way) to Millard Canyon Camp.

Maps: Trails Illustrated Maze District/Northeast Glen Canyon and USGS Turks Head, Cleopatra's Chair, and Horsethief Canyon.

Permits: Vehicle camping or at-large backpacking permit required. Day use allowed with no permit.

Minimum vehicle requirements: High-clearance four-wheel-drive.

Road condition: Conditions vary on this long stretch of road. Many sections are rocky and slow going, but nothing extreme. Just before you reach the river and Millard Canyon Camp and the Green River, the road gets very rocky.

Suitability for mountain biking: Good to excellent conditions most of the way with a few rocky sections, especially near the end where road heads down to the river.

Vehicle camps: Ekker Butte is not one of the prime campsites in the area. It's mostly slickrock, and tent camping is marginal. The NPS considers it an overflow site, so it's usually available. The Millard Canyon Camp is right on the Green River and is one of the nicest campsites in the Maze.

Special attractions: Great campsite on the Green River, and you probably will have the area to yourself.

25 SUNSET PASS

Total distance: From Waterhole Flat Junction, 4.5 miles (one way) to Glen Canyon NRA boundary.

Key points (from Waterhole Flat Junction):
- 2.5   Sunset Pass Camp.
- 4.5   Glen Canyon NRA boundary.

Time required: From Waterhole Flat Junction, 1-2 hours (one way) to Glen Canyon NRA boundary.

Maps: Trails Illustrated Maze District/Northeast Glen Canyon and USGS Clearwater Canyon.

Permits:	Vehicle camping or at-large backpacking permit required. Day use allowed without a permit.
Minimum vehicle requirements:	High-clearance four-wheel-drive.
Road conditions:	Packed dirt most of the way with a few short rocky sections and one long section just on the east side of the pass, which is actually a gap in the Orange Cliffs.
Suitability for mountain biking:	Excellent conditions with a moderately steep climb to the pass.
Vehicle camps:	Sunset Pass Camp is in a grove of junipers and pinyon pine on the south side of the road just as it goes through the gap in the Orange Cliffs. It's exposed to the wind and rain, but not nearly as much as popular campsites such as Maze Overlook or Standing Rock.

26 WATERHOLE FLAT

Total distance:	From the Flint Trail Junction, 6.5 miles (one way) to Waterhole Flat Junction.
Time required:	From Flint Trail Junction, 1 hour (one way) to Waterhole Flat Junction.
Maps:	Trails Illustrated Maze District/Northeast Glen Canyon and USGS Clearwater Canyon and Teapot Rock.
Permits:	Vehicle camping or at-large backpacking permit required. Day use allowed with no permit.
Minimum vehicle requirements:	High-clearance two-wheel-drive from Hite; high-clearance four-wheel-drive from Hans Flat Ranger Station.
Road conditions:	From the Flint Trail Junction to the Waterhole Flat Junction, it's packed dirt with a few short rocky sections but easy going all the way, especially the southernmost one-half of this section of road where it gets so good that you might have to be careful not to exceed the 15 mph speed limit. The north half goes between precipitous Red Cove on the east and massive Orange Cliffs on the west, both well-named for their color, and the south half goes across the broad, mostly flat terrain of Waterhole Flat. On some older maps, you may see a road heading west over to Sunset Pass, but that road has been recently abandoned. The same old map might show a road heading south down a wash to the Doll House Road. This looks like a shortcut, but it isn't an official road and probably takes longer than driving the long way

around. The long route is easy driving, and you can make great time compared to driving through the narrow, rocky wash.

Suitability for mountain biking: Excellent road for mountain biking.

---

27 THE ROAD TO THE DOLL HOUSE

Total distance: From Waterhole Flat Junction, 21 miles (one way) to the Doll House.

Key points (from Waterhole Flat Junction):

3.6   Teapot Rock Camp.
9.2   Golden Stairs Trailhead.
10.3 Canyonlands National Park boundary.
13.8 The Wall Camp.
15.8 Standing Rock Camp.
17.1 Chimney Rock Camp.
17.2 Harvest Scene Trailhead.
20.6 Turn to Doll House 3 Camp.
20.7 Colorado/Green River Overlook Trailhead.
20.8 Spanish Bottom and Granary Trailhead.
21.0 Doll House 1 and 2 Camps.

Time required: From Waterhole Flat Junction, 3-4 hours (one way) to the Doll House.

Maps: Trails Illustrated Maze District/Northeast Glen Canyon and USGS Teapot Rock, Elaterite Basin and Spanish Bottom.

The Chocolate Drops dominate the horizon from the Maze Overlook camps and trailhead.

Permits:	Vehicle camping or at-large backpacking permit required. Day use allowed without a permit.
Minimum vehicle requirements:	High-clearance four-wheel-drive.
Road conditions:	From the Waterhole Flat Junction, the road starts out smooth and stays that way for about 3 miles. Then, it gradually gets rougher as you approach the Teapot Rock Camp. After passing by the campsite, you face a 5-mile section of road that is probably the worst in the Maze District, and you probably can walk it faster than you can drive it.. You must get out of your vehicle frequently to check routes over ledges and in rocky sections. Use extreme caution all the way unless you want to seriously damage your vehicle and get stranded in the Maze. After you reach the Wall Camp, the road gets better, turning into mostly packed sand with a few rocky sections. From Chimney Rock to the Doll House, the road has sections of loose sand and gets seriously rocky just before the Doll House.
Suitability for mountain biking:	Conditions may be better for mountain biking than they are for driving, especially in the section from Teapot Rock Camp to The Wall Camp. After the Chimney Rock Camp, the road has some sections of loose sand. Some loose sand and rocky sections may prove difficult for novice riders, but for the most part, this is a fantastic mountain biking road.
Hiking:	Note trail descriptions for Golden Stairs, Harvest Scene, Colorado/Green River Overlook, Spanish Bottom, and the Granary.
Vehicle camps:	Vehicle camps in the Maze do not have vault toilets. You are required to have a portable toilet with you. **Teapot Rock Camp** — The road goes right by this camp, so privacy can be a problem. Plus it's very rocky and exposed, but it does have a great view of Teapot Rock. Also, if you don't have a high-clearance four-wheel-drive vehicle, you can camp here and hike or mountain bike into the Maze area. **The Wall Camp** — On the north side of the road about 100 yards off the road. Very scenic campsite with great view of the Maze, Chocolate Drops, Standing Rock and many other famous formations. Very exposed, so it can be unpleasant on a windy day. **Standing Rock** — Right in the shadow of awesome Standing Rock, so you can sit in camp for hours and wonder how this smokestack-like sandstone spire survived the power of nature. Like The Wall, this camp is about 100 yards north of the road and is quite exposed.

The Doll House.

Chimney Rock — Following the trend set by The Wall and Standing Rock, this camp is just north of the road and very exposed, but has incredible scenery. It has the attraction of being right by a major trailhead for trails and off-trail routes into the Maze and serves as a base camp for hikers who like day hiking instead of backpacking.

Doll House 1 — Semi-protected between two massive sandstone towers, but still with a good view off to the east. Close to the trailheads for designated trails leaving the Doll House area. This camp, along with the other two Doll House camps, has the advantage of privacy, since all these are located at the end of spur roads.

Doll House 2 — Like Camp 1, Camp 2 is tucked amidst of the Doll House towers. More exposed than Camp 1, which can be a problem on windier days, but less exposed than Camp 3.

Doll House 3 — Unlike Camp 1 and 2, you can get a great view of the Doll House itself from Camp 3. It's in an open area on the southwest edge of the famous sandstone formation. This can be the least desirable of the three on a windy day, but the most desirable in good weather. Also, Camp 3 is farther from the official trailheads for the three designated trails leaving the Doll House area.

Special attractions: Truly spectacular scenery and the aura of remoteness and self-reliance.

Special precautions: Hazardous road.

28 HITE

Total distance:	From Waterhole Flat Junction, 32 miles (one way) to Hite.
Time required:	From Waterhole Flat Junction, 2-3 hours (one way) to Hite.
Maps:	Trails Illustrated Maze District/Northeast Glen Canyon and USGS Clearwater Canyon and Bowdie Canyon West.
Minimum vehicle requirements:	High-clearance two-wheel-drive.
Road conditions:	With the exception of a few rocky sections near the Waterhole Flat Junction, this is a two-wheel-drive road all the way to the paved road just before Hite.
Suitability for mountain biking:	Excellent conditions for mountain biking, but not quite as scenic as many other roads in the Maze.

ABOUT THE AUTHOR

The author taking a break at a spring on Syncline Loop Trail in the Island in the Sky District of Canyonlands National Park.

LIVING ONE MILE AT A TIME

Whenever Bill Schneider isn't out in the wilderness, he wants to be. He has spent more than thirty years hiking trails all across America.

During college in the late 1960s, he worked on a trail crew in Glacier National Park. He then spent the 1970s publishing the *Montana Outdoors* magazine for the Montana Department of Fish, Wildlife & Parks and covering as many miles of trails as possible on weekends and holidays.

In 1979, Bill and his partner, Mike Sample, created Falcon Press Publishing Company and released two guidebooks that first year. Bill wrote one of them, *Hiking Montana*, which is still popular. Since then, he has written eleven more books and many magazine articles on wildlife, outdoor recreation, and environmental issues. Along the way, on a part-time basis over a span of 12 years, Bill has taught classes on bicycling, backpacking, no-trace camping, and hiking in bear country for the Yellowstone Institute, a nonprofit educational organization in Yellowstone National Park.

Today, Bill still serves as publisher of Falcon Press Publishing, which is now established as a premier publisher of recreational guidebooks with more than 350 titles in print.

FALCON GUIDES ® Leading the Way™

• *To order any of these books, check with your local bookseller
or call The Globe Pequot Press at (800) 243–0495.
Visit us on the World Wide Web at:*
www.falcon.com

FALCON®

BACKCOUNTRY ZONES

HORSESHOE CANYON UNIT

GLEN

CANYON

NATIONAL

RECREATION

AREA

ISLAND IN THE SKY

CANYONLANDS NATIONAL PARK

THE MAZE

THE NEEDLES

BACKCOUNTRY ZONES

MAZE & ORANGE CLIFFS
M-1 Maze Area
M-2 Orange Cliffs
M-3 High Spur

Note: The Green and Colorado Rivers are also zone boundaries.

ISLAND DISTRICT
I-1 Day use area
I-2 White Rim
I-3 Taylor Canyon
I-4 Syncline
I-5 Upper West Basin
I-6 Lower Basins
I-7 Gooseberry/Lathrop
I-8 Murphy Point

NEEDLES DISTRICT
N-1 Day use area
N-2 Davis and Lavender
N-3 Upper Salt
N-4 Salt and Horse
N-5 Butler/West Side Canyons
N-6 Red Lake/Grabens
N-7 Needles Trails
N-8 Needles North

- – · – · – National Park / N.R.A. boundary
- ~~~~~~ Planning area boundary
- ········· Zone boundary
- Front country zone
- ▦▦▦ Closed to camping

- Closed to entry seasonally
- Closed to entry
- ——— Paved road
- ——— Unpaved 2-wheel drive road
- ········· Unpaved 4-wheel drive road

- ········· Trail
- ⊥ Permit required for vehicle entry
- ⌂ Campground
- ▲ Primitive campsite
- 🛈 Ranger station

N

Please carry a topographic map for backcountry travel. Canyonlands terrain is rugged and may be impassable.

Cartography by TRAILS ILLUSTRATED